THE COUNTRY VICAR

THE COUNTRY VICAR

Reshaping Rural Ministry

David Osborne

DARTON·LONGMAN + TODD

First published in 2004 by
Darton, Longman and Todd Ltd
1 Spencer Court
140–142 Wandsworth High Street
London SW18 4JJ

ISBN 0–232–52546–3

A catalogue record for this book is available from the British Library.

Designed by Sandie Boccacci
Set in Palatino and Stone Sans Italic by
Intype Libra Ltd
Printed and bound in Great Britain by
Page Bros, Norwich, Norfolk

Contents

A note about people and places
All the people and places mentioned in the short stories between the chapters are fictional. All the stories are based on real situations.

Acknowledgements

This book has been a long time in the making and I would like to thank all those who have helped in the process. They include all the churchwardens, Readers and other church members I have had the privilege to work with and who, together with my ordained colleagues, have helped me to do and to think about the work of a country vicar. I particularly want to thank David and Valerie Barrow for support and friendship in the early years; George Lovell and Catherine Widdicombe of *Avec* for their insights and skill in reflective analysis; Brian Woodcock and Steven Palmer for enabling me to understand better my own work and theirs through our consultancy meetings; Dick Acworth, for (often unwitting) insights into the life and work of an Archdeacon; Nigel Done, for introducing me to the work of Raymond Fung; Elizabeth Thomson for numerous suggestions about the text and for giving me a greater understanding of George Herbert; Susan Green, for ten years as a colleague and for showing me the potential of Reader ministry; and Madron for working, living and being with me the whole time.

To Madron

A Start: The Induction of Peter Fynn

Richard Cutter, Archdeacon of Trent, drained his teacup and thought of whisky. He had spoken to seven churchwardens after the service: an accountant, three housewives, a teacher, and two who had once been some kind of manager but were now retired. One from Leppingham had left as soon as the service was over.

The table in the centre of the hall was still well stocked with sausage rolls but all the fruitcake and quiche had gone, and the crowd was thinning. At the door the Reverend Peter Fynn was still greeting his new parishioners. Some slipped by whilst he was occupied with another, but many wanted to shake him by the hand and say something to explain who they were, or to try to make him feel welcome.

Sheila Edwards, sixtyish with a well-cut jacket and a sweet smile. 'Lovely to have a young vicar with a family. It will be so good to see younger people coming to church.' Peter's family had already left, Helen Fynn dragging two exhausted children back to the vicarage. They had been very quiet during the service. So quiet that Helen had at times been suspicious, but she had then decided that there was enough in the strangeness of this different church, the unknown congregation, the people walking around with water and bread, the ringing of the bell and the bishop taking his hat off and putting it on again, to keep them amused on this occasion.

Then Roger Jones, Chairman of Clound Parish Council, spoke to Peter, hoping that he would get involved in local affairs. 'Parish Council Meetings are on the first Monday of the month and it'll always be good to see you there.'

And Colin Macdonald, retired from the City at fifty and now operating some kind of money business from The Gables at Great Barwood. 'Call by, any time you are passing.'

A stocky woman in a blue polyester coat. 'I hope you are going to start confirmation classes. There are a lot of youngsters in the village needing confirmation.'

A thirty-something woman with frizzy hair. 'Will you be doing an Alpha course? My sister in High Wycombe did Alpha and it sounds fascinating.'

Reginald Grembell, retired canon of Salisbury now living in Dorminster, leant forward slightly and spoke quietly and clearly to Peter's shoulder. 'You need to visit. Essential. The clergy must visit.' And then he too moved away.

Richard noticed the bishop was still stuck in the corner. It now looked as if he had a couple of cathedral cognoscenti engaging him with talk of choirs they have known and loved. At least he had been able to move on from the local councillor who had been bending his ear about the bypass. For someone who was tone deaf the bishop could keep up a good conversation about church music.

The diocesan bishop wasn't likely to be here again. Maybe in a few years young Peter would have a confirmation, but then it would probably be one of the suffragan bishops who would come. The diocesan bishop had been here twice in the last twelve months, so would not expect to be here again however long he stayed in the diocese. He had been here last June for Basil Bradwell's funeral.

Richard Cutter could not place the woman now talking to Peter the Vicar. Ah, yes, an old people's home.

'I'm Mary White. I run The Elms at Shalton. You might have heard of us. We used to have our own little communion service every Tuesday. Reverend Wilkins from Dorminster used to come. I do so hope you'll be able to keep it up. Our people do so appreciate it.'

Peter made a sound which was both positive and non-committal, and Richard thought he was learning fast. Mary White continued. 'Of course, if Tuesday's not possible we could always change the day. Except Wednesday – the chiropodist comes on a Wednesday. And we do bingo on Thursday afternoon.'

It was like this after institution services. A large congregation in the church, to see the new vicar and, of course, the bishop, and then tea and cakes afterwards in the village hall. This was not bad as halls went. A 1920s job by the look of it. Possibly a memorial hall, and recently redecorated. Ageing, but solid. Probably a fair bit of money went into it from the Frontleys at Lower Barwood. At least that should mean that Peter wasn't involved with any trusteeship for the building. If the Frontleys were involved it would now be a strictly non-church affair. Ah, yes, a memorial plaque. And a picture of the Queen, in fading blue. One of the coronation editions. The teacups, 1950s pale green. Food spread on wooden folding tables. Perhaps also 1950s.

There was now a grey-haired man in tweed talking to Peter. 'Prayer Book,' the Archdeacon heard him say. 'It's never been the same since we gave up the Prayer Book.'

And then Bob Cradger, farmer from Shalton and former Vice-Chairman of the County NFU. 'What's needed here is a strong lead. No pussyfooting around. Get on with it. I knew a chap up Crimthorpe way who took over a church and within two years he'd filled it. Lead from the front.'

There was now an old lady at the front of Peter's queue. 'I'm Elsie Watcher,' she said, as if Peter was also deaf. 'And I was in the choir when the Reverend Bradwell was instituted. We all went up to the new vicarage afterwards for tea, and squash for the children. He was a wonderful man.'

An interesting word to use, thought Richard. Not the one he would have chosen, but then, Elsie knew him as a parishioner, not as his archdeacon.

Basil Bradwell had been instituted in 1963, when he was in his early forties. The old vicarage had been sold to a local solicitor and a new one built on the glebe beside the churchyard. And there Basil had stayed, saying his prayers morning and evening, visiting in the afternoons the elderly and the women who did not go to work, and holding occasional Church Council and school governors' meetings in the evening. His wife had died in 1984 and with his children far away Basil had developed no other life beyond the parish. He had typed the parish magazine till three years ago, when the former school secretary took it over. The church had been well maintained with the help of his churchwardens, one of whom, Percy Thrudden, had been warden for thirty of Basil's forty or so years in the parish. And they had eventually gone over to using a modern form of

3

service in 1985, after Bishop Walker summoned him to an interview at the palace. No one knows what the Bishop had said to him, but Walker was known for his frankness on occasion. Since then the Book of Common Prayer had been supplemented by a modern language communion service once a month.

But neither the Bishop nor the Archdeacon could do anything about Basil's retirement. Instituted when he was, when the compulsory retirement age came in it did not apply to Basil. He had the freehold of the living and could stay put. Which he did. Any attempts to persuade him to retire as he entered his mid-seventies were met with the question that if he was not here who would there be to care for the people of the parish. Great Barwood would be put in with other parishes. They would not have their own vicar to look after them.

Which was absolutely right. For years now the plan had been for Great Barwood to join with Shalton, Clound and Leppingham, to make one unit which was the size of a normal rural group of parishes now, but Basil would not budge. Shalton and Clound had been served from Dorminster, where there was an active retired vicar who was keen to help out, and Rodney Brown at Widderton had been Priest-in-Charge of Leppingham. It had made Rodney's into a group of six parishes but he was willing to help out for the short term. It was a short term which only ended when Basil suffered a stroke and went into a nursing home in Dorminster. Only then could he be persuaded to resign. And that had been hard. It was not that Basil thought he would fully recover. He knew he would not. But he was having to face the fact that he was approaching the end of his life.

Richard had visited him several times in the home in Dorminster during his last months. He had been able to speak, though with some difficulty, and his hearing had not been good in the last few years. On the first visits he was unwilling to put in his hearing aid and Richard had suspected it was because he did not want to listen to and talk with the Archdeacon. But as time went on he was willing to listen, and then wanted to talk. Slowly he came to accept that he would not be going back to the vicarage at Great Barwell. He was then concerned about where he would live when he left the hospital and Richard promised to find accommodation for him in the area. He was concerned about how he would manage with his now limited mobility, and Richard assured him that he could find somewhere for him where he would have the support he needed. But beyond these fundamental practical concerns there had been one more pressing and deeper theme, which rose to the surface on a number of occasions. Basil wanted absolution. He wanted to know that he was forgiven.

Not for holding up the diocese's reorganisation of his parish but for being such a bad vicar. Richard heard several times of the funeral that Basil had forgotten and arrived late for, of the way that there were now no children coming to the church, and of the old man whose hospital visit he had postponed till the next day, by which time the old man had died of another heart attack. He heard of the young woman who came twice to the church and then told him that she would go with her family to another church in Dorminster where, she said, there was some spiritual life. He heard of the argument which raged on in the Senior Citizens' club for three years and which he had not been able to resolve. He heard of how Basil had not prepared anyone for confirmation for the last six years.

Basil told of recent decline and past failures, of opportunities missed, and of an inability to run the courses and the prayer groups which the clergy from Dorminster talked about. Basil had ministered to his parishioners as he had been taught when he was a curate. He had said his prayers. He had read his Bible. But he had watched his church life decline, and though he had told himself that it was more important to be faithful than to be successful, he felt a failure. He felt responsible. And he felt guilty.

Richard had ministered to him as he could. Basil never moved into the sheltered housing in Widderton where Richard had arranged a place for him. Perhaps he had a peaceful death. His son had come over from the States and his daughter had come from Glasgow for his last few days. At the funeral service the Bishop had honoured him, telling of his example as a dedicated and self-sacrificing pastor.

Now the Bishop had spoken of new possibilities for the parishes with their young vicar, of the challenges of Christian faith in our time, and the encouragement of having young men and women coming forward for the ordained ministry.

And the congregation of Great Barwood thought of old Basil, and the elderly like Elsie Watcher thought of Basil in his young days, when he had been full of energy and dedication, out and about on his bicycle. And the congregation from Shalton, Clound and Leppingham were glad that the reorganisation they had waited for had at last come about and they had a young vicar who was committed to them and not just someone who, however good and caring, was not their own person.

So the matter of Great Barwell, which among many other things had occupied the Archdeacon's mind for some years, had at last been resolved. Richard put down his teacup and walked over to speak briefly to the bishop before passing the new, enthusiastic and tired vicar with a friendly word and going home to a glass of Glenlivet.

He knew something of the varying degrees of success with which the other clergy in his archdeaconry managed to swim around in their parishes' sea of hopes and expectations. It would be interesting to see how Peter Fynn got on.

1

The Country

For all its cities and rambling suburbs there is still a lot of countryside in England. Take the train from London to Newcastle and there is mile upon mile of open farmland. Drive from Birmingham to Plymouth and the motorway is bordered by farmland for all but a few miles passing Bristol. Even in the South East, walk from Guildford to Canterbury along the North Downs and the views to the south are of woodland and fields, with a few villages and small towns making an appearance amidst the green. It is all countryside and it is very varied. Broadleaf woodland, open downs, moorland, stonewalled dales, miles of open arable land and hedge-separated pastures spread across humps, hills and broad valleys. In the Thames Valley an incline of a hundred feet is known as a hill. In Cumbria it is not noticeable. In parts of Lincolnshire it would give views of twenty miles.

Rural industry
It is also largely an industrial landscape. There are small estates of manufacturing workshops scattered across England and in places, larger, more conspicuous factories. Old airfields have sometimes become haulage depots and ware-housing. Windfarms are becoming an increasingly common sight, and all the country's nuclear power stations are in the countryside. Large areas have been shaped by mining. Many of the spoil and slag heaps have been landscaped and grassed over, or even wooded, but in places the settlement patterns and placenames still tell tales of small pits scattered across the

coalfields. Quarrying has also reshaped the land in many areas, and some of the country's seaside resorts owe their origins to the fishing and transport industries.

But farming is, of course, the most noticeable industry in rural areas: 70 per cent of England is used for farming of one kind or another, though the kind of farming varies considerably from place to place. Sheep farming on fells is a very different business from growing vegetables on the Fens or producing milk in Devon. It is a different business in many ways: the working pattern, the skills required, the overheads, the capital investment needed, the financial support system, as well as the amount of land needed and the landscape it produces.

In most rural areas the farmers and farm workers are a small proportion of the population. The actual numbers will vary considerably according to the kind of farming carried out but in a village of three hundred people there might be only a couple of farms with five or six more in the few square miles around. Each farm might have a full-time staff of just one or two with contractors, a relief milker and a secretary making up the hours equivalent to another worker. That might be twenty people in all directly involved in farming operations out of the total population. There are less than 400,000 people employed in agriculture in England, a quarter of whom are part-time and seasonal workers.[1]

Other people work in businesses which are subsidiary to and dependent on agriculture: haulage, supplies and maintenance, building and accountancy; so what affects the farming industry affects many other people besides farmers. A quarter of the working population in rural England works in wholesaling, retailing, hotels and restaurants. When large parts of the countryside were closed off during the foot-and-mouth epidemic of 2001 it had a profound impact on many rural businesses.

Despite that fact that only a small proportion of the people in a country area work in farming, it is always the most visible industry in rural England. Farming is what people see going on around them. In a city it is possible for few people to know what actually goes on behind a factory wall or in an office but in the country people can always know something of what goes on on farms because they see it happening in the fields if they stop and look.

Population changes

A century ago there were many people in rural England who were not directly involved in farming even in a predominantly agricultural area. There were blacksmiths, hauliers, builders, quarrymen, shopkeepers and travelling traders, workers in sawmills and brickworks, roadmen and railway maintenance engineers. A village might have had a few professionals residing nearby who had offices in the local towns and also maybe a local industrialist who could now afford to live at some distance from his. There might have been a few families who lived off their rents or investments. But back then farming did occupy a lot more country people. Children were employed picking stones and scaring birds; cows were milked by hand, women turned the paddles to make butter; ploughing, harrowing, sowing, hoeing and reaping were done with horses or purely by hand, and everything had to be hauled in horsedrawn carts.

The biggest change came in the 1940s and 50s when tractors became increasingly widespread. In the thirty years since the Second World War an average of 20,000 fewer people each year was employed in agriculture.[2] In the 1980s, as ever bigger farm machines became available, an increasing amount of farm work was taken over by contractors. Now in an English village there might be one or two people who work not directly for a farmer but for a farming contractor or who are self-employed, hiring out their services and equipment and working over a wide area round about.

Some of those who once worked for farmers are now retired and others are unemployed. Many work in other local industries, in light engineering, haulage or security work, travelling to the local town or wherever the day's contracted work is located. Many of them do not regret the change. Farm work was never well paid and the hours were long. Those

9

who got out into other employment in times of growth rather than recession probably ended up with working conditions and pay which are still not good by national standards but are likely to be better than farm work ever was.

Old farm cottages are now often occupied by people who have moved in during the last few years. Who it is that has moved in will depend on how near the area is to the nearest town or city, its proximity to a motorway or a railway station, and the scenery. Anywhere within a few miles of a motorway exit will be attractive to city workers who want to live in the country and can afford the housing. Some villages have developed to become almost completely occupied by town or city commuters. There are thousands of villages in England where one or two farmers milk their cattle while a hundred other people take their cars along the lanes to join the main road or motorway to their work in the nearby city.

Most villages will have a population with a range of incomes and a variety of lifestyles. There will be some with incomes that are well above the national average, who have moved into the country but continue to work elsewhere. They might have a company car and possibly a newly built large house, a converted barn or 'Old Rose Cottage' which was once three dwellings but has now been converted into one residence. There might be lower-paid white-collar workers: teachers, middle management, local government employees, or others whose incomes are nearer to the national average but who have moved in wanting to be able to look at green fields, hear less traffic and have more garden and maybe somewhere they can keep a horse or a couple of sheep.

There might also be alternative lifestylers who grow their own organic vegetables, burn renewable fuels on a multi-fuel stove and recycle their organic waste through the compost bin. They are less likely to be where the houses are close together but in somewhere more remote, costing less but with more space for the vegetable garden and maybe chickens and a goat.

Also within or near a village there might be a number of people who have retired into the countryside. If they can afford it a lot of people move out of the city or the town when they retire. Where they move to will depend on a lot of factors of which scenery is one. Retired people have more time to look at the scenery than they did when they were working. But affordability is another factor and the two are often linked. Devon and Dorset are more expensive than the rural stretches of Nottinghamshire. But any rural part of the country is likely to have some retired people who never worked in the area but moved in when they finished work. Their likely background will vary according to the part of the country, its scenery, its amenities, and the associated price of property.

In any rural area there may also be some people who are just stopping over for a short while. Some places attract tourists and holidaymakers who swell the population many times over during the summer. They bring in money, fill up the roads, and put pressure on local services. They are welcomed by people in the tourist trade but sometimes treated with polite disdain or even loathing by those who think or wish the local economy could manage without them. There might also be travellers or Gypsies, perhaps using designated campsites but often simply parked up in a layby or by an old railway track. The area might have a nursing home, or an old army camp or college being used for housing asylum-seekers. It might also host a hospital, a prison, a military camp or an air force base.

Then, in most rural areas there are one or two very big houses. A hundred years ago each one was likely to have been the home of a local landowner with a staff of gardeners, grooms, cleaners, chambermaids, cooks and a butler. But during the first half of the twentieth century, and largely as a result of the wars and of death duties, property was sold and the new buyers were sometimes institutions, investment companies, financial houses, or wealthy dealers in international finance. Some of the big houses were completely unmanageable and fell down or were demolished. Others have become hotels, conference centres or residential homes for the elderly. Some are owned by very wealthy commuters. Some still remain in the hands of the same families who also own the land round about or have a substantial part in the trust which technically owns the estate. These are fewer than they were, but, in some parts of the country at least, they are still there and together with their agents provide another small but not insignificant element in the social mix which is rural England.

Somewhere in any cluster of villages and hamlets there will probably be a vicar. It is very unusual now for a country parish to have its own. The parishes of Shalton, Clound, Great Barwood and Leppingham do not exist, and neither does their new vicar, the Reverend Peter Fynn, but that is now the pattern. Unless they are remnants of another era, Basil Bradwells who managed to hang on against church re-organisation and increasing age, country vicars now have several parishes. Maybe four. Maybe only three. Sometimes as many as nine or ten. Rumour had it once that there was a vicar in Herefordshire with thirteen, and another in Lincolnshire with seventeen, but if they existed at all these were probably passing phases: interim arrangements awaiting the day when another Basil Bradwell would retire or pass away and a rather more rational linking of parishes could be introduced.

It was common a century ago, when there was the greatest number of clergy ever in the Church of England, for a country parish to have its own vicar. But during the twentieth century the number of clergy declined and in the 1970s there was a move to have proportionately more clergy in the cities. Whilst some rural clergy had had parishes of three hundred people some urban vicars had had twenty thousand. By the end of the twentieth century it was normal for a country vicar to work in four or more parishes with a total population of perhaps two thousand people. In areas of low population and small communities a vicar might have many more parishes, whereas a vicar of a market town might only have one or two very small parishes as well. Or it might be that now several clergy work together over a wide area. Like the landscape and the settlement pattern the way that clergy work varies from place to place.

What is 'rural'?

It is difficult to have a clear definition of what is meant by *rural* England. Anthony Russell has written about there being four types of countryside:[3] the urban shadow, accessible countryside, the less accessible countryside and remote or marginal countryside. This categorisation serves as a reminder that the countryside is diverse but it is not always obvious which category a particular area should go into. Accessibility depends on your means of travel. There are areas of Buckinghamshire or Suffolk which are very accessible from London if you have a car but not if you rely on public transport. Parts of Cumbria or Cornwall can feel like an urban shadow during the holiday seasons with roads as congested as any in East Kent or Berkshire, though they are a long way from any conurbation.

In this book I am using 'rural' to mean areas which when looked at on a map are largely farmland, moor or forest with separated settlements ranging from single dwellings to small towns. What constitutes a small town as distinct from a medium-sized town is again not clear-cut. A small town in Berkshire could be much bigger than a medium-sized town in Cornwall. Wokingham is bigger than Truro. In his 1966 study *Communities in Britain*[4] Ronald Frankenberg described Ashton in Yorkshire as 'a town that was a village'. His point was that in the town, which had fourteen thousand people when the study was made, people related to each other in a way more commonly found in villages. This book draws on the experiences and study of vicars working mostly in villages and their surrounding areas. In many towns and even parts of some cities some things will be similar.

Settlement patterns in the countryside vary considerably. Some people in the country live in isolated houses, others in hamlets, others in villages of various size and market towns and others in resorts. The facilities available and the social life of such communities varies considerably. Larger communities tend to be more vibrant. There is more going on that people can join because there are more like-minded people to do things with. This is the logic and it is borne out by studies of different communities, but it is not the whole story.[5] There are small towns which bustle with book fairs, concerts, exhibitions and markets and others in which little seems to go on. There are villages of three hundred people in which no one seems to know anyone else and others where people get on like a big family.

One reason for this is that in small communities a few people can make a big difference to the way that people relate to each other and to what they do. Anyone who has worked in small communities will be aware of the way in which one or two people can sometimes spread a wet blanket of gloom over any suggestion or activity, whilst others are able to make anyone feel part of the community within minutes. Villages can change quite quickly when a new family moves in or two or three people move away or die within a short period of time. In dealing with small communities it is hard to generalise, as individuals can make a big difference to the whole.

Another country

The present diversity of landscape and settlement pattern across rural England is the result of a variety of factors. These include the underlying rock structure, the way the land was shaped after the last ice age, the local climate and the history of land ownership and its use in the last few centuries. All these are likely to have been studied in some depth, both the major developments and small local matters like whether a nineteenth-century landowner was willing to have a railway across his estate, or who won in a twentieth-century argument about a small industrial development. Any county library will have this in its deeper shelves and a little of this might also be on the shelves of a larger bookshop.

But on the shelves of any bookshop in England there will certainly be books on 'English Country Villages', 'The Country Garden', 'Farmhouse Recipes' and 'Country Cottages'; every stationer will have 'country life' magazines and, in November, the 'Beautiful Britain' calendars will hit the shelves. These publications will have lots of pictures and it is likely that while they might show something of the diversity of small English settlements and of the cuisine in the farmhouses of previous generations they will show little that is not beautiful, colourful or appetising. These are not studies of rural England as it is. These photos of villages will be carefully angled or airbrushed to leave out the 1950s council housing and the pylons, the farmhouse tables will not have shredded wheat or cornflakes, and the gardens will never include an old bike and a pair of jeans on the line. These are books about another rural England: the one which is the focus of many people's thoughts about their home country, of their dreams for their retirement or the day they win the lottery.

In discussing a possible definition of what is rural the Countryside Agency suggests that while there are various different definitions in use by different agencies and organisations most people know the countryside when they see it.[6] That seems like a good way to proceed. However, a couple of years ago I had a visit from an aunt who had lived for most of her life in an English city. After lunch we went out for a walk, down the hill, past the ford and then up a lane under overarching hawthorns with stone cottages behind.

'Oh, this is very like the country,' she said.

The only thing I could reply was, 'Well, it *is* the country.' We were in the genuine article. I live in a village in Somerset which is surrounded by fields and has a population of less than a thousand. The nearest town is three miles away, and that only has eight thousand people. But her point was not only that it was countryside but that it looked like countryside. For her, country was a matter of appearance, as it was for one of my neighbours I once met out for a walk. In our conversation he explained how his wife had been disappointed after they moved in because she had been expecting there to be lots of nice country walks and there weren't any.

He was, of course, out for a walk in the country but as far as his wife was concerned a country walk meant something in particular, and this place did not have it. Maybe she wanted leafy lanes, bedded with dried autumn leaves, and meadows with gambolling lambs or open moorland and deep wooded valleys with rushing streams. There are certainly quiet lanes and patches of woodland, but it was clearly not countryside as she thought it ought to be.

Rural England is not only a reality, the major part of the country in terms of land area, but it is also a myth. It is an idea that shapes people's thinking and influences their emotions. This myth is an aggregate of symbols and stories and provides the backdrop for light dramas and comedies. The mythical rural England has a pub by a village green, shire horses and duck ponds, cottages with wisteria, and roses and hollyhocks in the garden. Houses there are thatched or tiled (but preferably not slated) and built of stone or warm red brick (and not pebbledashed). The pace of life is slower, there is cricket and darts (rather than football and pool) and time to chat to one's neighbours.

This is the rural England that sells tubs of margarine and wholemeal bread. It is protected by societies against so-called development and it is part of our heritage. It is glimpsed on holidays and is a place for retirement or recuperation. It is a restful place and one where people are at ease with themselves and with each other. This rural England is populated by people who live in communities, not just neighbourhoods, where they look out for each other, and where they will pull together if things get tough.

In this rural England people live in villages and in each village there is a church. In the 'Beautiful Britain' calendar a photo of an English village will normally include a church tower providing both height to the composition of the picture, a sense of history and a spiritual dimension. Wales has castles, Scotland has mountains, lochs and men in kilts playing bagpipes. England has villages with pubs and churches.

And somewhere in the mythical village, together with the retired colonel and one or two colourful local characters, there is also a vicar. The vicar possibly rides a bike. The vicar may be elderly, middle-aged or young, trendy and good with the young people, but the vicar knows everyone and has time to chat and to visit. And the vicar looks after the church.

The clash of myth and reality

Sometimes the myth and the realities of rural England clash with each other. A couple on their retirement move from the Birmingham suburbs to Exmoor where they had many happy holidays. After eighteen months one is ill. Maybe the other does not drive. It is November. There are no buses. The few neighbours are at work all day, or the nearby houses are only occupied in the summer by holidaymakers. Shops, surgeries, hospitals and banks are all some distance away. A daughter might drive down from Solihull: two hours down the motorway and another hour and a half for the last forty miles.

A company director moves to Dorset planning to drive up the A303 to Basingstoke several times a week and finds that every time he arrives there his car has to be washed to remove cow muck that is freshly spread across the lanes twice a day.

A village is divided between those who want street lights in the place where they have always lived, and those who have moved in and think street lighting is not appropriate in the country. Or between those who want the local quarry extended because it will mean continuing local employment, and those whose prime concern is the noise, the dust and the traffic. Or between those who want a housing association to put up small homes which their sons and daughters might be able to afford to live in, and those who think any further development will spoil the village.

This clash of myth and reality also affects the vicar. Since *The Vicar of Dibley* entered the national psyche it is now widely accepted that the country vicar might be a woman. *The Archers* has had a woman vicar and the 2004 BBC documentary *A Seaside Parish* followed the work of Christine Musser, a woman priest in Cornwall. But many of the expectations of the country vicar are based not on the reality of the countryside or of the church in the twenty-first century but on the rural England of many people's imaginations.

This book is about real country vicars. These vicars are often seen at church services and occasionally at village events. Some local people will know the vicar. Others will not. Some do not want to.

Being a vicar at the beginning of the twenty-first century is very different from how it was in the early 1960s. The countryside has not been left behind by the cultural changes that have affected the cities and the suburbs. The work of vicars has changed significantly in the last forty years and being the vicar of four or more parishes is not the same as being the vicar of one.

This book is about country vicars and how they can do their work in the rural church as it really is. If the Church of England is to operate effectively in the rural parts of the country its members need to think realistically about its clergy, and that is as true of lay church members as it is of bishops and diocesan administrators. The aim of this book is to contribute to that thinking and to move it along.

Though there are far fewer country vicars than there were forty years ago the book focuses on the country vicar not as an endangered species but as a continuing key player in the life of the church. It looks at what country vicars do, at the pressures they are under and at the unrealistic ideas and expectations they have to live and work with. But more importantly it suggests a way forward not just for the country clergy but for the rural churches of which they are a part. It is intended for anyone who is involved or interested in the life of the church in the countryside.

The book focuses on the Church of England although I believe that much of what I am suggesting here is of relevance to other denominations as well. I also believe that whilst it focuses on the life and work of the country vicar it is also relevant to the work of clergy in cities, towns and suburbs. Many of the issues that rural churches and their clergy have to address are not confined to the countryside but face the church in many other parts of the country as well.

There never was a time when every parish in rural England had its own resident vicar. This was an aspiration of the church in the late nineteenth century but it was never realised and by the 1920s rural parishes were beginning to be clustered into small groups sharing a vicar.[7] Now this is the prospect for some urban parishes as well. At the same time diocesan managers are having to deal with what appears to be an increase in stress-related disorders and dysfunctions among the clergy.

Some in the Church would like to redesign the whole organisation on the basis that the Church of England as it has developed over the centuries is not structured to address the challenges of this century. However, the Church of England has procedures and checks and balances which mean that whilst it continually changes it always changes slowly. There is currently a loosening up of some structures to enable the Church to develop modes of operation which are more suited to the ways that people of the present time relate and socialise.[8] What I am suggesting here is not something that first requires a radical restructuring of the Church but a way of working within the current structures. In due course these will change. They will have to. But the church in the country-side cannot wait around until that has happened. There are issues which the church in the countryside needs to address now, for its own health and for the well-being of society.

With a concern for the whole church and for society this book focuses on the work of the country vicar and addresses the question of how country vicars might think about and understand their work in such a way that they can handle the pressures and remain constructive towards the church, their communities and themselves, balance their own needs with the demands and expectations of others, and retain their vision and passion for the gospel.

A Vicar in the Village

'Why on earth is the vicarage here?' asked Archdeacon Richard Cutter.

He had found it again eventually. He had driven round the village looking for it and found it eventually in the corner of a field with a garden separated off by a rusty chain-link fence. From the gate a drive stretched eighty yards to the front door. But behind the house there was obviously only a small back garden.

'Why is the vicarage set so far back off the road?' said the vicar. 'Or why is it at this point in the village? Or why is it in Pratley at all? Have you not been here before?'

'Yes, once to see Hugh Pritchard, your predecessor, and once during the vacancy when we did some work on it. But I always forget how to find it and I've often wondered.'

'Well, they built it when they sold off the old vicarage – that big place down beside the church. It's now owned by an antique dealer. I think the locals couldn't face the thought of their vicar not living in a grand house so they got the smaller vicarage built with a long impressive drive. Except it's not impressive, it's a pain. There's all this grass and you can't even run sheep on it because someone'll leave the gate open and they'll be eating everyone's bedding plants before we can catch up with them.

'But I think they put it in this corner of this field because it was the nearest bit of glebe land to the church.'

'But why's it in Pratley? It's not the most obvious place to have the vicarage in this benefice.'

'No, the sensible place would be Ashworth. That's where most of the people live. There are fifteen hundred people in Ashworth, a school, a couple of shops and a bus service. Here there are fifty houses, no shop and no buses.

'Fortunately my wife drives. She works in Dorminster. And our children are living away now. But for Hugh, with his young family and his wife unable to drive, it must have been very hard. For them as much as for him.

'But the patron of Pratley lives in the parish at Plumbwell Park and I've heard from one of the churchwardens that every time the diocese has proposed joining more parishes together the patron here has dug his heels in and said he'd only agree with it if the vicar lived in Pratley.

'He's also made sure there's never been a pub in the village. He's very concerned for the welfare of his villagers, is our patron. No pub and a vicar in the village.'

'But he doesn't actually live in the village himself?'

'Oh no. But we see him from time to time. He comes to Matins.'

'But what about the other villages?'

'Ah, they're not his. He doesn't own the farms and he's not the patron of the livings. He's looking after his own.'

'As one does. Remind me. Who are the other patrons who go along with this?'

'If I remember rightly, Breadney is the Society of St Perpetua, Grapton is Sir John Courtenay who lives near Hereford, Hawkham is the trustees of Lady Eleanor Whimple, Notley is Porton College, Cambridge and the patron of Ashworth is the bishop.'

2

The Vicar

What is a vicar?

While it is possible to work with a fairly loose definition of 'countryside', and even the Countryside Commission is willing to do that, we need to be clearer when we are thinking about the vicar. The word 'vicar' has three different meanings.

First, the word is applied loosely to anyone who is ordained. Methodist ministers and Catholic priests will all be called 'vicar' on occasions. Anyone who wears a clerical collar might be referred to as a vicar. Much of what I am suggesting here is relevant to ministers and churches of other denominations. Much of what Church of England clergy experience is also experienced by others. Many of the issues they face are the same and the churches have a great deal in common. But there are some features of life for a Church of England minister which are different and this book is principally concerned with Church of England ministers.

The second meaning of the term 'vicar' is a very specific and technical one within the Church of England. In the Middle Ages the clergy had two sources of income. The first was land which had been set aside by a local lord for the parish priest's use and was known as glebe. The priest would initially farm it himself although as time went on it became increasingly common to let it out. The second source of income was tithe: a tenth of the produce of all the land in a parish. Around the year 1000 this tithe was divided into four parts, one for the local priest, one for the bishop, one for the maintenance of the church building and one for the relief of the poor. However the situation changed so that the tithe eventually came completely to the parish priest who then distributed the revenue as he saw fit. The tithe was a payment in kind, including livestock as well as crops, which the priest could sell. It was effectively a local tax to pay for the church minister and building and for the support of the poor.

In this way there began two institutions: the living, which consisted of the glebe and the tithe, and patronage, which was the right to appoint the parish priest which passed on from the initial donor of the land to his descendants. In time these institutions changed their form. First the entitlement to the tithe sometimes passed to another person or organisation, like a monastery, a college, or a bishop. They were the 'rector', who had the right to the tithe, and they then set aside some of the income to pay a 'vicar' who represented them in the parish. The incomes of rectors and vicars varied considerably according to the wealth of the parish. Second, in time the patron might come to be someone who had little connection with the place. The patron might be an individual, but it might be an organisation, like a college, or it might be the bishop. Patronages were sometimes sold and in the eighteenth and nineteenth centuries societies within the church bought up patronages so that they could put in one of their own kind of people as the vicar: a Catholic or an Evangelical of a particular style.

Through the nineteenth and twentieth centuries the tithe had first been changed to a financial levy on landowners and then been abolished. From 1978 onwards all glebe rents and investment incomes were handled centrally by the diocesan administration and by the Church Commissioners, and clergy were paid a standard diocesan stipend. There remained anomalies and cathedral staff, bishops and archdeacons received bigger stipends, but vicars within a diocese were basically on a flat rate. This might vary from diocese to diocese but there was a nationally agreed minimum stipend. With glebe rents being handled centrally there was effectively no difference between a vicar and a rector as far as the minister or the people of the parish were concerned, although the different terms remain in place. Many country clergy are the vicar of several parishes and the rector of others, in which case they are titled 'The Rector'.

Patronage remains, though it was changed by law in 1986 so that, among other things, representatives of the local congregation were able to veto the appointment of a vicar. The practice is that a patron presents someone to the bishop to become the vicar or rector of a parish and if the bishop or the local representatives do not object the bishop appoints this person. They are then the incumbent of the living. They do not have a contract but have some freehold rights with regard to the church and the vicarage or rectory and are entitled to a stipend which is paid by the Church Commissioners from money passed to them by the diocese. Dioceses in turn obtain most of their income from local churches.

The third use of the term vicar is less technical and refers to anyone who is in charge of a Church of England parish. Now many people who are referred to as 'the vicar' are not actually legally vicars or rectors. They are not incumbents. When a vicar leaves the bishop might decide to suspend the living. A legal process is followed which means that the patron is not able to present someone to the bishop to become the vicar, but the bishop can appoint a priest-in-charge of the parish. The suspension is only for a limited period of time, but it can be renewed and it gives bishops flexibility in reorganising parishes. It means a priest can be given responsibility for a parish while other changes are made in the parishes around and while parishes can be clustered in new ways or reorganised. So sometimes a person might be the incumbent of one or two parishes and the priest-in-charge of others. A retired priest might be put in charge of a parish on the basis that they will not work full-time in the parish and will not be paid, but will have the use of the vicarage free of charge. This is generally known as a house-for-duty arrangement.

There are also priests-in-charge who have other part-time jobs. The other job might be other work for the church such as advising in rural affairs, communications or in clergy selection or training. It might be something completely different such as building, teaching or running a business. This vicar might previously have worked full-time as a parish priest before this appointment but they might never have done so, coming to take on responsibility for a group of parishes from a period of non-stipendiary, or voluntary, ordained ministry.

Since the 1980s there has been a considerable development of non-stipendiary ordained ministry: clergy who undertake their work in the church in a voluntary capacity, supporting themselves and their families with another occupation. Sometimes they see the other work as principally a way to support themselves for their church work. Others see themselves as having two professions, that of teacher, vet, doctor or whatever, and a priest. Some see their ordination as adding another dimension to their principal occupation and to their lives. Sometimes a non-stipendiary priest might be given responsibility for a group of parishes and continue to do this church work voluntarily.

As far as most people in the parish are concerned it makes little difference to them whether their local Church of England minister has the freehold or is a priest-in-charge, whether this minister receives a stipend or does it voluntarily. As far as they are concerned this person is their vicar. They might find it interesting if this person does another job as well but they will still be 'the vicar' if they are the ordained Church of England minister in charge. It is in this third sense that I am using the term 'vicar' in this book. The vicar is the person who has the principal responsibility for the ministry of the Church of England in that parish.

Teams of ministers

Since 1968 there has been a development of group and team ministries. In a group ministry several clergy, each with their own areas of responsibility, work together. In a team ministry a large cluster of parishes will have several clergy working within them. In a team ministry the team leader will be styled the Team Rector and the others Team Vicars. Team ministries have had varying degrees of success over the years. Some having operated for some years have now been disbanded but others continue.[1] A group of country parishes could therefore have several 'vicars'.

But in many groups of parishes where there is not a formal team the vicar does not work alone. There might also be other ordained ministers who do church work on a non-stipendiary, or voluntary, basis. Some of these might work full-time at other jobs but still give some time to parish work.

In a group of country parishes there might also be a curate. The term 'curate' used to refer to anyone who was an ordained parish minister: who had 'the cure (or care) of souls'. So it is that in the *Book of Common Prayer* Holy Communion Service the congregation prays for bishops and 'curates' but says nothing of vicars. The vicar was the curate and another ordained minister who helped them was the Assistant Curate. But now the use of the word has changed and assistants are generally now known simply as 'curates'. Curates are usually people who have completed an initial period of theological study, been ordained and are now working with a vicar to gain experience of parish work and to continue their training. Everyone ordained in the Church of England is expected to do at least three years as a curate in a parish. They might then go on to become the vicar of another parish or a chaplain with their own area of responsibility or they might become a non-stipendiary minister somewhere.

The vicar might also work with a number of licensed lay ministers. The most numerous of these are Readers. The office of Reader was invented in 1866 for men who would be authorised by the bishop to read morning and evening prayer but the role developed considerably over the next hundred years. By the middle of the twentieth century Readers were assisting at Holy Communion, preaching, and undertaking a wide range of work across parishes under the direction of the vicar. Women first became Readers in 1969. By 2000 there were more Readers than parish clergy in the Church of England. So while it is possible that in a group of country parishes there might be another ordained minister apart from the vicar, it is quite likely that there will be a Reader or two. The Reader might have a full-time job while putting some time into church work: leading services, preaching, visiting, taking funerals, preparing people for baptism or confirmation, leading study groups or doing administrative work for the church. The Reader might be retired from other work and contributing a great amount of time to the church's ministry.

There might be other licensed lay workers who have trained in a different way. Readers are trained within their diocese, normally doing three years of part-time study and then a period working with their vicar. There are also schemes whereby people train nationally for full-time lay church work. The first deaconesses in the Church of England were members of a community founded in 1861. There were never many of them and in 1987 women were able to be ordained deacon and in 1994 ordained priest. By 2003 15 per cent of Church of England clergy were women. Deaconesses no longer feature in the church's published statistics but there are other licensed lay workers, particularly officers of the Church Army.[2]

Some dioceses, like Peterborough, have developed schemes for training and authorising other lay church workers such as Pastoral Assistants. Others, like Lichfield, have developed the scheme for training and licensing Readers so that a Reader might be licensed with the expectation that their principal work in the church will be leading worship and preaching but it might instead be teaching in study groups or in pastoral visiting or youth work.

One point of such schemes is that they mean the people undertaking this kind of church work have had a basic level of training, they are clearly responsible to their vicar and to the bishop, and can be recognised by parishioners as representing the church in what they do. A drawback of such schemes is that church members can feel that they cannot lead worship, visit neighbours on behalf of the church or lead study groups unless they have the necessary training and piece of paper. On the one hand it is a rule of the Church of England that an ordained minister cannot operate as such within a diocese without the bishop's permission, whether by licence or some other form of written permission, and these schemes extend that principle to lay church members. On the other hand the Church of England also has a long tradition of having lay church members, such as Sunday School teachers and youth workers, doing very significant church work simply on the authority of the vicar. So there will be some parishes where there are a number of licensed lay workers of various sorts and others where there are none. In the latter it might be that the vicar is expected to do all the church work but it might be that there are a number of lay church members doing all sorts of things from baptism preparation and leading children's clubs to visiting the bereaved. They may have had some training, they will do these things with the vicar's authority and in accord with the church's policy for the protection of children and other vulnerable people, but they are not licensed as Readers or some other kind of official lay minister.

In some dioceses there are also some Locally Ordained Ministers. A Locally Ordained Minister is someone who has undergone some training, been ordained and is therefore able to celebrate Holy Communion, to baptise, to conduct weddings and do all that another priest might do, but is licensed on the basis that they will only do this in a particular locality and as part of a ministry team. Some dioceses have developed Locally Ordained Ministry while others have not. Only priests can take Holy Communion services. Readers and other lay people cannot, so this is a system which has considerable attractions for rural areas where there might be a large number of parishes grouped together with several ministers but only one priest. But in some dioceses there is considerable caution about this development on the basis that it creates a two-tier system of ordained ministry.

There is no clear picture as to how this will develop in the long term, but something has to happen. In the foreseeable future there will be a continuing reduction in the number of clergy. The number of people offering themselves for the ordained ministry, being selected, trained and ordained is not keeping pace with the number who are retiring. In the rural areas this will mean bigger groups of parishes sharing the decreasing number of priests. But also during the twentieth century, while the number of ordained ministers was diminishing there also developed an expectation in much of the church that Holy Communion would be a regular feature of church worship. So something has to give. There are various options. One is less frequent Holy Communion services. Another is fewer churches. Another is authorising more people apart from those who have been through the full theological training to preside at the Holy Communion. Another option is church services at different times during the week. There are various options available but things remaining the same is not one of them.

Groups of parishes

The whole of England is divided into Church of England parishes and the periods of time when a parish does not have a vicar are still seen as exceptions rather than the norm, however long they are. People can expect to have a vicar whether they want one or not. The vicar may be full-time, part-time, house-for-duty or a volunteer and might work with a Reader or two and maybe a clergy volunteer. On the other hand there might be no other authorised ministers in the parishes and the vicar might expect or be expected to do all the work of parish ministry alone.

The number of parishes the country vicar has will depend on several factors, including the spread of population and the local history. For a vicar to have four parishes with a total population of two thousand is quite normal, but there are considerable variations. In some parts of the country it might take over twenty parishes to make up a population like that, in which case a vicar's total parish population may be less. In other areas the settlement pattern might be of small towns of perhaps three thousand people with surrounding villages of a few hundred. There the population of a cluster of parishes is likely to be considerably more, and the number of churches less. Even if the church authorities had a free hand there would be no way of sharing out parishes so that there was an even spread among the clergy.[3]

It is expected that the number of clergy will decrease further in the next decade. Whilst it is hard to predict how many people will be trained for and enter the ordained ministry it is known that a large number are due to retire in that time. There are also serious constraints on how many the church can afford to employ. In many areas parishes will be reorganised into larger groups.

However, the Church of England is only able to reorganise parishes when a vicar chooses to move or agrees to take on more, and then it can only be done with local consultation and a measure of agreement. Bishops, archdeacons and others involved in the process may well want to bear in mind the different needs of different parishes, as far as they can ascertain what those are. They may have difficulty working that out. But they will have to respond to the demands of the local congregations, and also of the patrons of the parishes. The long and complicated history of the church means that the reorganisation of parishes is not a simple affair. Nevertheless, it has proceeded, if only at the pace of an elderly snail, for two hundred years, and it still continues. The clergy are spread across the country and each parish, at least most of the time, has a church minister whom people will generally refer to as their vicar.

Pastoral work

It is likely that this vicar would be welcome in some of the houses in these parishes if the vicar was able or chose to call round. Many houses would be empty during the day. There would be some where the people were interested that the vicar called but also slightly embarrassed. Apart from offering the vicar a cup of tea what do you do? Some people would wish the vicar would call at another time, although they might not be able to think when that would be because their lives do not have much space for entertaining random callers. Others really would not want a vicar to call round on them at any time.

Some would welcome a call from the vicar to offer encouragement, to show the church cared, to offer prayer and maybe practical advice, or simply as a mark of solidarity with them in a personal difficulty. Sometimes vicars are involved in their parishioners' significant personal crises. Many families, perhaps most in rural areas, want the involvement of the church when someone dies. The vicar may be one of the first people to hear what has happened although often it will be a phone call from a funeral director. A funeral may take three or four hours of a vicar's time, including a visit beforehand, a service and a burial in the churchyard. The vicar may also visit the family afterwards. But a funeral can take a lot longer, involving several meetings with the bereaved family, a service, a visit to the crematorium which is perhaps thirty miles away, interring the ashes afterwards, and possibly a later memorial service. This can take fifteen hours or more altogether.

There are some people who haven't yet died but are seriously thinking about dying and who would like some of the vicar's time. It may be that the vicar will have some insight which will help them. It might be that because the vicar is often dealing with this the vicar is one person who can speak clearly and without embarrassment about what is happening, and that can be a help.

There are other serious crises in which a vicar might be involved: the birth of a seriously disabled child, an accident, a marriage breakdown or violence in the home, a missing child, a redundancy or bankruptcy. These are the kind of things where someone may want another person to talk to who is not personally involved, but may not need a professional counsellor or therapist.

Apart from crises a country vicar is likely to be welcome at various points in community life. Many parish councils would not think it strange if the vicar attended meetings and some would welcome it. Some vicars become members of the local civil government. Fundraising events, barbeques, fetes, old people's clubs, history societies, amateur drama groups, social clubs and political parties are all likely to welcome the vicar's attendance or membership. And many vicars welcome these opportunities, not least because it means that if and when they do end up dealing with a family in a crisis they are not dealing with strangers. They might also feel they have a particular contribution to make to the events.

There are, of course, the happy events for which vicars are called in, or those which are at least meant to be happy. A lot of rural weddings take place in churches, and the likelihood is that if one of the couple has a home in a village and the other is from a city the wedding will happen in the village. The offspring of villagers, now away most of the time working elsewhere, will often want to be married in the village church. At a minimum a wedding is likely to involve the vicar in a discussion with the couple concerned about what they are actually doing in getting married, taking down essential details for the marriage registers and a conversation and some phone calls to sort out music and hymns, organists, bell-ringers and others, a walk through before the actual event and then the service itself. Sometimes if the wedding is big or complicated there will be more conversations and phone calls.

People sometimes like to celebrate other events with a church service. Fifty years of being married, or a reaffirmation of marriage vows, perhaps after a period of coolness or a repaired breakdown, or just because they feel like it. And there are baptisms. Often these are seen as a family event, a kind of welcome and naming ceremony, although they are seen by the church as fundamentally a religious event, as the induction of a person into church membership. Usually the person is a child, but not necessarily so. People can be baptised at any age. Baptism calls for some explanation on the vicar's part and some careful handling. There are clergy who come to rural ministry from urban situations where only regular churchgoers have their children baptised, and who have strong views about the need for people to demonstrate their allegiance to Christ by regular churchgoing. They can find themselves in a minefield if they are seen by parishioners as putting up barriers and obstacles to the baptism of a village child.

Worship

All this happens within a framework of regular church worship. Generally every Sunday every parish church will have a service. Some will have two. And most congregations will want a service at an accessible time on a Sunday morning: some time between nine and midday. So in a rural group of three parishes the vicar is going to be hard pressed to do them all. With five or more it is impossible. Services then have to be led by other people: Readers, retired clergy, non-stipendiary clergy or lay members of the congregation who do it with the vicar's support. This will involve the vicar in preparing a plan and asking all these volunteers whether they can take particular services, making sure they have the necessary resources, perhaps choosing hymns and making it known what the set readings are, finding other people to help in doing Bible readings, leading prayers or maybe contributing to the worship in other ways, making sure the churches are prepared for the services with heat, light, candles and anything else they need, and keeping in touch with the local church leaders in order to know what is going on week by week. Each church has two churchwardens and often others who will also take a part in ensuring that worship happens in their church.

The framework of worship has its more basic level when day by day the vicar is likely to be in one of the churches for prayer, maybe with one or two other parishioners. There are also the high spots when bigger celebrations are called for. Advent Sunday kicks it off, with perhaps a special service for the season, and then there is Christmas. Most villages want a carol service, maybe a crib service, and certainly a Holy Communion service or two. Few vicars with four parishes would get away with less than twelve services going on in the week-long run up to Christmas dinner. And then it is New Year, an excellent time for a service of reflection on past and future and maybe for joining with the local Methodists for their Covenant Service. This will be followed by Epiphany and (or) the celebration of the baptism of Jesus. Four weeks later it is Candlemas, an opportunity for imaginative worship with children, perhaps a Christingle if there has not been one already; and then it is Ash Wednesday and Lent, Palm Sunday, with palms and a donkey for the strong hearted, and Holy Week leading to Good Friday meditations, and everyone wants a bright and beautiful Easter celebration, which again has to be Holy Communion.

Then the village becomes preoccupied with summer. Rogation Sunday gives a chance for outdoor worship at farms or beating the bounds, Ascension Day might be an opportunity for something different in the local school, Pentecost is crucial to the church's story of itself but is now generally ignored by all but the regular congregation, and the long weeks after Trinity are liturgically fallow, giving a pause for breath before harvest festivals and Remembrance Sunday, and Advent once again. In holiday resorts where the residents are often working longer hours, summer services might be geared towards holidaymakers, some of whom may only come to church when they are away from home.

In 2000 when the Church of England scrapped its Alternative Service Book and introduced *Common Worship* it decided that one book for all occasions was not what the church needed, so it introduced a small library of worship resources, with options and variations, templates, outlines and explanations of the structure of a liturgy. The result was that all over the country local churches produced their own service books which drew from the material provided and more or less complied with the regulations. Usually the vicar did much of the work involved. The outcome was ten thousand services which were similar but of which no two were identical. And week by week there will be some variations to the local established order of service. All this calls for preparation. Services out of a prayer book are now not common even on an ordinary Sunday.

Popular festivals call for bigger and more imaginative things than the normal variations on the Sunday service: plays, candles, flowers, marrows and baskets, flags, processions – all these might have their part through the year, together with music. Such services cannot be produced by cutting and pasting the texts in *Common Worship* but call for other resources and different ideas. Sometimes a vicar will plan these together with other people who perhaps work with young people, or are the members of a local club, or are a small working party formed for the occasion. Services also usually need hymns and other music. The vicar may leave the selection of hymns to an organist or to another trusted lay church member but some vicars feel they want to keep their hand on this, particularly as most people pick up what they believe, or think they believe, from what they sing rather than from sermons or prayers.

Preaching and teaching

Sermons are also a part of the weekly pattern of worship. Every church is supposed to have one every Sunday and vicars prepare them and preach. Usually when a vicar has several churches the same basic sermon can be preached in each one, but sometimes the vicar needs to address an issue which is specific to one community. There may be a local crisis, a bereavement, accident, or serious illness. It may be a local festival, or a service involving children, while in another church later that morning the service is likely to be solely adults. Vicars prepare their sermons in different ways. Some need a period of time in the study with theological reference books and maybe the computer. Others will mull over their theme and work out a sermon while they are driving around during the week.

Vicars also sometimes lead evening classes, Bible study groups, contemplative prayer groups and book groups, or try to ensure that other people are able to provide opportunities for study and discussion among their congregations. Vicars are also involved in schools. A large number of schools in rural areas are Church of England schools and the local vicar will almost invariably be a governor. The vicar may also take assemblies or even teach.

Administration and management

There is also work that needs to be done to keep the whole thing going. Every parish has a parochial church council, or PCC, of which the vicar is the chair, although some vicars leave the vice-chairman or chairwoman to actually conduct meetings apart from the annual one in which reports are given and elections, or selections, take place. PCC meetings are supposed to consider all church matters, and will certainly deal with matters to do with the church building and the finances, for which they have responsibility. In the week-by-week running of these things the churchwardens will play a key part. There have been churchwardens for centuries and a parish church cannot operate without them. The vicar may wish to have regular meetings with the churchwardens. This is more easily said than done because the vicar and church-wardens might live several miles apart; churchwardens are often at work during the week and are often not able to be at church every Sunday; the vicar of four churches probably cannot be at every church every week either and often needs to move speedily on to the next church after the service anyway. It is possible for a country vicar to go for several weeks without having a chance to talk with one of the church-wardens.

In every parish, even if there are no Readers or other clergy, there will also be a number of other people involved in doing church work. During the twentieth century an idea of lay ministry developed in many parishes. This was a shift from thinking of the work of the church as being what the vicar did to its being what the congregation did. Some of that would be the work of maintaining or developing the pattern of worship and prayer and the pastoral links and support within the parish, as well as the work with children or in study groups, maintaining the building and generally keeping the whole thing going. A vicar with five parishes cannot do what a vicar with only one could do. And most parishes in the last decade have had no vicar at all for some of the time and then either lay church members did things or they didn't happen. The vicar's work therefore often now involves keeping in touch with these people, offering support or advice if they need it or putting them in touch with other people who can give it. It may mean facilitating meetings of people across their parishes involved in a similar kind of work and leading or arranging training for people: children's workers, parish visitors, worship leaders and assistants, church treasurers and secretaries and churchwardens.

But there are phones, computers and e-mail. There is also printed paper and letters, and the vicar is for many people the doorway to the Church. However hard a vicar tries it is still likely that more church correspondence will come to or emanate from the vicar than the PCC secretary. Other levels of church management will generally communicate with the vicar. The address and phone number of the diocesan office will be imprinted in the vicar's mind within weeks of arriving in a parish. And there are other church organisations, pressure groups, campaign groups and organisations which exist to encourage and support, to stimulate change and encourage mission in local churches, as well as monumental masons wanting to put up gravestones, people trying to trace their ancestors, architects who are working on church buildings, organ tuners, upset parishioners, researchers with their questionnaires and the inevitable sales promotions. All these want to communicate with the vicar. There is also money to deal with: church fees for several separate parishes, divided between the parish and the vicar, and the vicar's portion to be sent on to the diocese or later deducted from the stipend, all require careful accounting.

Then there is the press. Some clergy hate and fear the press. Others use it. But if the press, radio or TV want a church representative for a quote they will ask the vicar, whether it be on a multiple bereavement, a paedophile youth worker, a hundredth birthday or a local rock festival. And vicars need to respond. Churches will also usually have their own publications. There are not many parishes which do not have their own magazine, and these are widely read. Sometimes the vicar will simply write a thought for the month and leave others to get on with it. Some vicars end up printing the thing themselves and organising the small army of distributors.

Beyond the parishes

The vicar is also one of the local churches' key links with the wider church and is seen by many people as a representative of that wider church. The clergy in the local area, the deanery, meet regularly in chapters, or are supposed to. Some opt out as much as they can but many find these a helpful gathering, if only to let off steam about their parishes, the diocese, or both. One of the local vicars will be the Rural Dean, having the kind of ill-defined role in which the Church of England specialises, but with a general brief of trying to make sure everything is going OK or even improving in the churches, and being legally the priest-in-charge if there is no vicar for a time. In some places that can be a long time.

Vicars will sometimes serve on diocesan boards, committees and synods, be members of other church organisations, meet with their counterparts in other denominations and sometimes work closely with them. They will try to keep up to date on what is happening in the Church, the world and perhaps also academia. They might campaign for fair trade, play in folk bands or orchestras, attend conferences, ride with the hunt, campaign against bloodsports, or write books. Somewhere amidst all this they probably have a family and certainly need friends, even when it is all going well.

The Resignation

Bob Heskell had written from his holiday to ask for an appointment with the Archdeacon as soon as possible after his return. Richard Cutter had decided to send a message to say that he would be late for the Board of Education, which seemed the least important engagement that week. He had now heard what it was all about: Bob had decided he was leaving parish ministry.

'How long have you been thinking about this?'

'About a year.'

'And praying about it?'

Bob paused. 'And praying. Yes. But that's not easy. Vicars aren't meant to give up, are they?'

'I don't know. Maybe some are. A vocation might change.'

'I'm not thinking vocation. I'm thinking about life. I've just been away for three weeks. Previous years I went away for two weeks in the summer but I found I spent the first week thinking about what I'd left and the second week thinking about what I was going back to. So this year I took three weeks. One on my own and then Sue joined me for the next two. And in the middle week I realised I was missing my life. I used to have weekends, and evenings off.'

'What did you do before you were ordained?'

'I was an engineer. I worked for a small firm that made equipment for the oil industry. Before that I worked for a large outfit. Sometimes we'd have to work long hours when we had a deadline to meet, but then there was space. Time off. Holidays. There's no time off in this job. The only holidays are when you go away.

'It struck me a few weeks before I went on holiday. I had a day off and felt like going for a walk. There's good walks round Crucksley.

But I was afraid that if I just went out for a walk I'd meet someone I knew. So I got in the car. That's crazy! Your own home's like a prison.

'Except it's not your home. It's the office. I go out to a meeting and as I'm driving back I'm wondering what's going to be on the answerphone when I get there.

'But you know all this. You've done it. And your job now is probably much the same.'

'Do you use an answerphone when you're in, to give yourself a bit of space?'

'Yes. On my day off, and at meal times. But even then you hear it ring. You wonder what it is.'

'So what brought this to a head?'

'The Annual Meeting in Crucksley. I was asked why we didn't sing the National Anthem on Remembrance Sunday. I explained that before my first Remembrance Sunday in Crucksley six years ago I'd met with the British Legion officers to talk about the service and explained that we wouldn't be singing the National Anthem because I didn't think it was appropriate when we were remembering people who had died in conflicts between nations. And they accepted that. So we haven't done it since then.

'Then after six years someone brought it up at the Annual Meeting. So I said we would discuss it at the next PCC.

'At the PCC I was told that a number of people were very upset about it. I wanted to have a discussion about why we should or should not sing it. They wouldn't do that. It was just what people wanted. They would not discuss reasons. And I said that we couldn't just do things on the basis of what people felt like.

'So then I had two resignations from the PCC. And a bloke called Ted Armitage wrote a letter to a number of people in the parish about how he'd fought in the war and some of his friends had died and I was dishonouring their memory.

'He never sent a copy to me so I can only go on what other people have said. He has refused even to talk to me. He won't even pass the time of day.

'So I spoke to the Chairman of the British Legion and asked to meet with them to discuss it, and he refused. He said they weren't going to meet just to have me tell them what to do. And he couldn't *conceive of the idea that I might want to talk it over with them and find some kind of solution.'*

'But you said you'd met with them when you first went there?'

'I did. But they now say they don't remember it. It obviously wasn't a big issue at the time. I've been there six years.

'I don't do the service every year, mind. I take one in Loppisham on alternate years. And Mary thought that one of the retired clergy who help in Crucksley had had the National Anthem sung one year. Maybe twice.'

'So someone has stirred things up, perhaps.'

'Possibly Ted Armitage.'

The Archdeacon thought about a time when he was a vicar in Manchester and a churchwarden had resigned and stopped coming to church. The church had then moved forwards in leaps and bounds. He'd only seen the man once after that, in Tesco.

'Where does he live, this Ted Armitage?'

'Three doors from the vicarage.'

'Too close for comfort in a village, I imagine. But he must be getting on a bit. You can't just weather the storm?'

'I'm not willing to.' Bob hesitated for a moment as if wondering whether to continue, then decided. 'It seems there was a Conservative Association garden party and people were talking about this. The MP was there and said he'd take it up. The next thing I knew I had a letter from the bishop asking me what was happening. He'd heard from the MP.

'So I wrote a long letter telling the bishop the whole story from my angle. Next thing I have the bishop taking me to one side over coffee at the diocesan synod and telling me how he wasn't going to tell me what to do on this, but that I had to remember that we were an established church and that he had to get along with the MP.

'So I thought about it, and on holiday I decided I just wasn't willing to put up with this any longer. I'm going to resign my living.'

'You don't think you ought to talk about it with the bishop first?'

'He didn't want to discuss the issue with me. He didn't invite me to come and talk about it with him. A quick word over coffee. That was all I got. With no recognition that it was bloody difficult for me back in the parish. If he didn't want to talk with me then why should

I talk with him now that I'm leaving. Except, of course, that I might need a reference!'

The Archdeacon thought for a while. 'I think I can probably see to that. What are you going to do?'

'Go back to engineering if I can. I've been out of it ten years, but it might be possible. I trained on the South Midlands scheme while I was doing my day job. Fifteen hours of study a week. And I sometimes thought it would have been easier to go to college full-time. But that would have meant I was even longer out of engineering, and things change fast.'

'What does Mary do?'

'She's currently a care manager with Social Services. She could probably get a job somewhere else in the same line.'

'And your children?'

'One at university. One finished now. They're standing on their own two feet. They've got their student debts which are bigger than they would have been if I'd stayed in engineering. But there we go. We all make mistakes.

'But I haven't resigned yet. I still need somewhere to live and a job until I can get myself sorted. When I do resign I'll write to the bishop and copy it to you.

'We've got a house in Redditch which we've let so when that becomes free we'll have somewhere to live.

'I feel sorry for these people who haven't got a house. It's all very well having a scheme to help retired clergy buy houses but what about anyone else who wants to go back into normal life? Unless, of course, you couldn't stand women priests. Then you got a golden handshake when you left!

'If the diocese was an engineering firm, or any other organisation for that matter, we'd be talking about stress at work. But who do you talk to here? The human resources manager? Who's that? The bishop?'

The Archdeacon didn't ask if he belonged to the union. 'You can talk to the Counselling Adviser.'

'Yes. That might have been helpful. But she's not going to change the system, is she?'

Richard left a space in the conversation, then asked, 'So you think it was a mistake being ordained?'

'I don't know. I'm not resigning my orders. At least not at the moment. And maybe I'll do some non-stipendiary work some time in some other diocese. I haven't lost my faith. Not in God, anyway. I'm sure God's in it somewhere. Somehow.'

'And you don't know how?'

'No. It's strange. I've had this image from Pilgrim's Progress in my mind since I decided to resign. When I look forwards now I feel like Pilgrim laying his burden at the foot of the cross and setting out on his journey. When I look back I feel as if I was being crucified.'

3

Pressures

Ministry in the countryside

Within one day's work a vicar might well talk with and listen to a grieving family, a couple who are excited about their new home, an elderly man who is seriously worried about the results of some medical tests, a middle-aged woman concerned about her mother's dementia and a group of excited young schoolchildren in a classroom. The day might also include chairing a meeting at which there is considerable tension or outright disagreement, fielding phone calls, any one of which might be from a parishioner who believes the vicar is doing things the wrong way or from a family that is waiting for mother to die, and spending some time trying to get to the bottom of a correspondence pile and the end of a job list left over from a church council meeting the previous week. Behind this the vicar might be turning over ideas for a sermon the following Sunday or a special service in a fortnight. All this calls for a wide range of skills and the mental agility so as to be able to respond appropriately to very different situations in quick succession.

This is true of any church minister of any denomination. Some pressures simply come from the nature of the job. Some come from the particular context, be it in a city, the suburbs, a town or the countryside. Some come from the structure of the particular organisation. Some come from history as that affects people's expectations of themselves and of other people. It is not my intention to compare systematically the ways in which clergy working in different situations come under pressure. My focus is on the work of country vicars and in describing that I am not suggesting that it is harder or easier than the work of other clergy. It is different in many respects but there will also be similarities. A vicar in a group of country parishes might find that a colleague working in an inner-city parish has to deal with some similar issues, as might a Methodist minister or Catholic priest in a town. In other respects the work will be different and different people doing similar jobs will feel pressure at different points depending on their personalities.

Country vicars might sometimes have an advantage over their colleagues in urban settings. The scenery might be good. Despite the idea that everyone loves the countryside, some people do not, but it is unlikely that anyone would end up as a country vicar if they couldn't stand the country. There are plenty of city jobs going for those that like or need the buzz of urban life. Much of rural England never makes it to the glossy books and calendars, but to those who like the space, hills or big skies, hedges and trees or long views across open land, there will in most places be some scenery which can, on occasion, give an emotional lift. It might be the big view. It might be the detail. But it is likely to be there somewhere. And some country vicars are even able to stop their car, look out of the window, and remind themselves that people come on holiday to look at this.

However, as those who move into the countryside after a working life of rural holidays soon discover, there are draw-backs simply with living there. Poor public transport means that if a couple are both to work they usually need to run two cars. The vicar cannot manage without one and it is almost certain that if their partner is to work they will need one too. And while for some professionals work is easy to get, for some other partners it can be difficult or poorly paid. Some can end up with little money left after paying for the car they need to get there.

There are not usually shops just round the corner. Many village shops have gone. Those that remain are usually more expensive and more limited than an urban cornershop. The vicar's family may feel a responsibility to use it, on the 'use it or lose it' principle. That pushes up the cost of rural living further. People who like to be able to go to the theatre or cinema, or listen to concerts, may find this involves long journeys.

Children can be isolated. A small village is likely to have few children. It is quite possible that in a village school there is only one child in a particular age group. Even if there are three or four they may have little in common. At secondary school they can have a wider circle and parents can find themselves spending a lot of time transporting their teenagers around the county so they can socialise. I was once a governor of a village school in which the chair of the PTA explained in tears that she was going to have to send her child to another school. He was the only boy in his year group and was desperately lonely.

But these are all hazards or drawbacks of rural living. They affect everyone who lives there. Living anywhere has its drawbacks. Living in the countryside has some advantages, if you like that kind of thing. Working as a vicar in the country-side has some particular challenges, some of which are the result of developments in church life in the last few decades.

Working in a cluster of parishes has some benefits. It means that in all but one of the parishes there is not a resident vicar, so church members are less likely to assume the vicar will do everything. Many country clergy find that it is the parish in which they live which seems to expect the most of them. In the other parishes people will just pick up the slates after a storm and contact the local builder. Where the vicar lives they tell the vicar there has been some damage. In the other parishes they call round on an elderly neighbour. In the home parish they assume the vicar will do it.

It also means that if there is one parish in which church life is going badly, there might be others in which it is OK. The minister of one church has all the eggs in one basket. The country vicar also lives a few miles from most parishioners. That means they have to be visited by car or on a bike, unless there is an uncharacteristic surfeit of time giving the vicar an opportunity for a country walk. It also means that parishioners are not likely to call round so much themselves without an appointment. The phone is much quicker.

Many vicars like having callers. Some do not like the phone. Certainly some kinds of conversation are best face to face, when the expressions and body language are visible. They say so much more. Sometimes it is necessary to just call by. An appointment makes the call a bigger event, and may even generate anxiety. Many sales reps are aware they sometimes need to drive fifty miles in order to happen to be passing a client. But the national culture has changed. Many very good friends or family members would not dream of calling on each other without phoning first. This is as true in the country as it is anywhere else.

There certainly are places where neighbours will just call in on each other, for a cup of tea, to borrow the lawnmower, or just for a chat. But the vicarage is likely to be set back from the cottages and council houses, with a drive, and it will certainly look different. It is sometimes conspicuous, sometimes hidden away. It is rarely just another home as far as those people are concerned who do just drop in on each other unannounced.

So while the vicar of five parishes lives at the office this home-based working is probably more characterised by phone calls all day and at all hours than by a stream of visitors. And the judicious use of an answerphone can enable a certain amount of control over the immediate demands.

People and communities

Possibly the biggest downside of having a cluster of parishes comes from not being able to be at each church every Sunday. This may not be a problem as far as the parishioners are concerned. The Readers or retired clergy may be better preachers than the vicar, they might take the service more in the way parishioners want, and people may not want to see the vicar too often. But for the vicar, who feels some sense of responsibility for what is going on in the churches, it can be difficult. The vicar doesn't know what is going on, or know who is there half the time. The vicar can no longer make a mental note that

Mrs Baggins has not been for three weeks, which is uncharacteristic, or that Mr Gumge is looking particularly frail, or
that the simmering row between the organist and the churchwarden has flared up again. The vicar depends on being told.

There are two opposing tendencies for the rural vicar. On
the one hand they are the vicar of their several parishes. And
they are seen as being the vicar by many people. They are not
just a vicar, or a minister. They are the vicar. *Their* vicar even.
And this means that in many ways country vicars are still
relating to whole communities. They are welcome to or even
expected to be at local events, and to take an interest in what
is happening, not just to their church regulars but to
everyone.

At the same time this everyone is a lot of people. Rural
clusters of parishes are not large compared with the population of an urban parish, perhaps two thousand compared to
eight thousand. But in the urban parish the vicar is often not
expected to relate to everyone and the whole community. In
villages that expectation is still there. Or the opportunity is
still there, and many rural clergy want to take it. It fits in with
what they see the church as being about. But they are very
stretched in trying to do it, not just by their diary, with the
perpetual problem of trying to spread themselves around and
fit everything in, but by numbers.

Some people have exceptional memories for names and
faces. But few people can have meaningful relationships with
a large number of people. A lot of work was done on this in
the sixties, which led to restructuring of large organisations.
The managers of big comprehensive schools soon found they
had to break the school into small units, and the teachers discovered they could not even recognise the faces of all the
pupils in the school, let alone remember their names. Soaps,
even if set in a city, have a relatively small cast. This is not just
because of the expense of paying a lot of actors but because
viewers lose a storyline if too many people are involved.
Novelists know this to be true. They can't keep the story
running if there are too many people involved.

In the recent TV documentaries on country clergy, *A*

Country Parish[1] and *A Seaside Parish*,[2] the programmes showed the vicar's pastoral involvement with a few people: estranged twins, a woman who had lost her dog, a bereaved woman who joined the church choir and a divorced couple. In each case this was followed over a series of programmes, giving a sense of the continuing nature of this kind of work that vicars do. But the programmes only showed these ones. More, and the programmes would have been overloaded and confusing. But these vicars would actually have had several such relationships running. Any vicar is likely to be involved at any one time with a number of people in this kind of way.

If a country vicar appears in a soap or drama they are either a minor part, enabling the writers to give the character an extended life in other places, as in *The Archers*, or they have only one focal community, which might be entertaining, as in Dibley or Balleykissangel, but which is quite unrealistic. The real country vicar is stretched across several, often quite separate, communities and maintaining a number of continuing pastoral relationships, most of which diminish in time but are replaced by others.

The vicar is also probably trying to be the principal church pastor to separate groups within each community, with their different attitudes, histories and assumptions: the farmers and the commuting executives, the occupants of the council houses and those at the Old Rectory and the Big House, the local hunt and those who oppose it or grumble about it, the Conservatives, the Liberals and the Labour Party, those who want a bypass and those who oppose it, the ones who expect everyone to join in village life and those who want to be left alone, the lovers of the old *Book of Common Prayer* and those who think services should be up to date, the ones who have lived there for ever and those who have just moved in. Each parish has its divisions and fault lines and trying to be the minister to them all can take its emotional toll.

Multiple congregations

Each parish will also, of course, have its church life. People have different views, preferences and needs regarding the type and style of worship they prefer or find helpful. Some vicars will limit the choice and only do (say) one form of Holy Communion, and a kind of service of hymns, readings and prayers which is meant to be accessible to all ages, usually called a Family Service. Others might restrict the services to the old Prayer Book or to the recent *Common Worship* options. But some will try to cater for as wide a range of preferences as possible, and maybe encourage people to try something with which they are not familiar. All this calls for a certain degree of liturgical dexterity as well as good organisation, particularly when they are trying to provide a range of forms of service in four or more different parishes.

Some vicars will decide they cannot really service several congregations, so they work to create one which moves week by week to a different church building: a sort of liturgical roadshow. People who want to go to church must travel to the parish where church is this week. Arrangements can be made to give lifts to those without transport or to share cars and cut costs. It means that after a service the vicar can stay and talk with people, not needing to leave for another church. It also means that a Sunday service stands a fair chance of having more than two dozen people. When the church arrives in your parish the building might be full. But then there is no service there for several weeks. Church worship is also very dependent on the vicar. With this system, church is where the vicar is.

An alternative approach, which is taken by the majority of country clergy, is to try to support each separate church. This supporting may mean struggling to keep each one going. It might mean helping them as they grow in size and confidence. It means drawing up rotas, training worship leaders, and sometimes bringing in retired clergy and Readers from nearby towns if they are available. It means keeping in touch with the churchwardens and other church leaders about what is happening in each congregation and parish.

But for the parishioners this means that they have a service available in their church every week, and the local regular congregation often grow in confidence when they realise they don't actually need a vicar to have a service. But there are not usually many of them when they meet together for worship and it can be dispiriting if week by week the congregation rarely hits double figures. This is particularly so if they have the expectation which many newcomers have who move into villages and have belonged to suburban churches, that church services ought to be lively and vibrant. Some villagers would love their church to have a music group and choir, a children's club and youth group, drama and dance, and all the things they hear about elsewhere, but there are just not the people to do them. In some places there still would not be enough people if the whole population were involved.

Quality and change

Parishioners who are not regularly at church also have their expectations. Some will expect church to be like it was when they last went, however long ago that was. Others will expect it to have changed, and they may or may not expect to like the changes. But there are problems with the simple fact of change in religion. Religious practice involves thought, imagination, emotion and memory. It taps into the depths of the psyche and employs symbols with all their associations and echoes. Religion changes. It has always changed, and what is sometimes felt to be timeless was once a novelty. People often forget that when the *Book of Common Prayer* was introduced there were riots in some places about this innovation. Handling change is a delicate but essential task for a vicar. Trying to introduce required liturgical changes, new ideas or different hymns is not straightforward. Ideally it needs time and good communication. That can be hard when the vicar is trying to service several disparate congregations.

There are also the expectations that people have regarding festivals and the special occasional services. A nativity play with children can get by however badly it is done, at least as far as the parents are concerned. They are not coming for quality but to see their child looking angelic. And that is what they will see. But for other people on other occasions expectations can be high. Professional musicians now find it

51

harder to perform to people's expectations because the audience are used to the digitally mastered and doctored CDs. Live music cannot reach the same standard of production, even though the expression may be better. Similarly people are used to quality performances on television, a frequent change of focus and voice, songs well sung and instruments well played. It might be that a city church with extensive musical resources, a large regular congregation and perhaps power-point technology can compete with this, but village churches cannot do so. And while people will make some allowances, of the kind they make for the amateur drama group, that it is OK because it is local, some will still find the village carol service or harvest festival disappointing.

Cathedral congregations are generally getting bigger, especially for festal occasions like carol services, as are some town and city churches which are large to start with. Many village congregations are holding their own, or declining. One factor in this may be that in a culture of entertainment rather than participation the churches that do well are those with the big resources. However, some small congregations are growing and in these cases it seems to be the personal nature of the small group that is attractive and helpful. This is a possible strength of a village church.

Money

Another feature of church life now which is significant for the clergy is the fact that congregations effectively pay for them. For several decades now congregations through their PCCs have contributed to diocesan funds what has been called variously a 'parish share' or 'diocesan quota'. This goes into the diocesan funds out of which the clergy are paid. In the last twenty years this has increased considerably to the extent that now on average what is contributed by parishes is the amount that is needed to pay for clergy stipends, housing and pension contributions. The Church Commissioners' contributions to the church's funding is now largely towards pension payments, bishops and archdeacons, cathedral staff and some support for the least well-off dioceses.

Even if nothing is said about this by the lay church members it is harder now for parish clergy to maintain a sense that they are somehow sent in there by the bishop and are not answerable to the congregation for how they work and what they do. It is not direct, but the people in the congregation are the ones who are paying their stipend. And the amount they contribute to the running of the church is quite considerable, apart from the time and skills they put in. In Bath and Wells Diocese in 2004 a rural church with thirty people who quite often attend can be paying a parish share of £9,000: £6 each per week. This is not a lot compared to the housekeeping or even the price of a round of drinks, but it is a lot more than the sub for the WI.

That only accounts for the cost of the clergy and the diocesan administration. The congregation are also paying to maintain, heat and repair the building, and for the other running costs of church life. If in 2004 a congregation can draw on the support of other parishioners for help with the building maintenance costs and perhaps each year have a major fundraising event they can possibly stay afloat for £8 per week each. This cost is projected to increase above the rate of inflation. It can be argued they will still be getting a good deal, but the important point for the parish clergy is that for some in the congregation this is significant money. No longer are churchgoers dropping a few coins in the collection while the vicar is supported from legacies of previous generations or by a kind benefactor. The congregation are contributing noticeable money towards the cost of their church.

The vicar is also contributing significantly, not least with time and skills. The work calls for a variety of skills, it involves a long training, the clergy generally work long hours and are not highly paid. The vicar needs to be able to deal with people, to listen, to speak publicly, chair meetings, and be competent at accounts and administration. The work requires adult teaching skills, and a knowledge of the law and practice of the church. Behind this, though, if the vicar is going to do any more than simply keep the show on the road, there needs to be a spirituality and a theology. Some parish

53

clergy would see themselves as the neighbourhood theologian. They might not talk about God all the time but they need the ability to hear and think about matters and contribute on the basis of what they believe about God and the world. This comes through study and through prayer. And this prayer needs to be not just a matter of saying the words but something that affects their personality and roots them in the God they speak about.

The selection of potential clergy is normally a long and careful process. Many who think this is their vocation are told otherwise somewhere along the line. But if selected, this is only for training, which can take up to three years. It used to be that all potential clergy went to a theological college, but many now undertake theological study through a part-time course whilst maintaining their present job. Then, after two or three years, they are ordained and work as a curate, or trainee minister, under the supervision of a vicar. After at least three years as a curate they might become a vicar. Before ordination they receive no pay from the church. If they are at a residential college they will receive small grants to support themselves and their family. Once they are ordained some clergy support themselves by other work but normally vicars are paid a stipend. In 2004 this is likely to be about £18,000 plus the use of a house rent free. The church has an aspiration to eventually raise this to what £20,000 would have meant in 2003, although many doubt that the church will actually do this. Even with that, for most people becoming a vicar involves earning less than they would in a similar profession requiring the same level of education and training.

The employment status of the clergy is currently under review and undergoing change. It would be good to be able to say that the change is coming about through the church realising that having its clergy notionally employed only by God was a little unsatisfactory, but in fact the change is being brought about by European employment legislation. Vicars do not have contracts of employment. Some have job protection based on centuries-old legislation, a situation known as the clergy freehold. Others have licences from the bishop which have some of the status of a contract, but also a degree of uncertainty with regard to renewal or possible termination.

Like some other professionals vicars are exempt from the European working hours regulations. If they work more than 48 hours a week they are not committing an offence. Most of them work much more. Studies in 1990 and 1998 both showed the clergy to be on average spending 56 hours a week on work and work-related activities.[3] Since 1990 there has been increasing concern about clergy exhaustion, stress and burnout, though there is no evidence that they work any less now. And it may be that some of the stressors have increased.

Confused expectations

One of the biggest stressors is the lack of clarity about what is expected of the vicar. Country vicars have their own ideas of what they think they should be doing. Parishioners also have their view and it is not necessarily the same, and is probably never voiced, apart from in a tone of disappointment that it isn't happening. Some of what the vicar actually wants might be impossible in four or more parishes. And then there are the initiatives and ideas that come from elsewhere.

Bishops, diocesan officers and various organisations are frequently exhorting the vicar to greater emphasis on the church's mission, rather than simply maintaining the institution. They even have lots of ideas about how it should be done, or what it would look like if it were happening – known as 'the marks of mission'. There are others who exhort the vicar to focus on the educational aspect of their work: teaching adults, organising housegroups, preparing people for marriage, or baptism, training local leaders. Others encourage a more ad hoc approach to things, with plenty of slack time for just talking with people at the school gate or in the pub, being known and seen about the place and taking opportunities as they arise for encouraging a growth in faith. Others have a sense that the standard of worship is poor and want to help the clergy and others make it more meaningful, or lively, or imaginative. Others have a sense that the crucial thing is the vicar's own spirituality so that he or she can help others in their own spiritual quest.

Vicars also have their own personal agendas. One way or another they have families, friends, maybe dependants, possibly elderly parents. They have their own interests, be they trains, butterflies or jazz, and their own needs. Food, sleep and sex are as much a part of vicars' lives as they are anyone else's.

When a vicar starts work in a parish there is a grand service, known variously as an induction, institution, licensing, or the slightly less esoteric 'celebration of a new ministry'. There is at least an archdeacon and maybe a bishop, hymns, a big congregation, clergy from the surrounding area, friends and wellwishers, perhaps a coach load from the previous parish. A solemn moment in the whole proceedings is when the bishop, in full regalia, or the archdeacon on the bishop's behalf, hands the vicar a piece of paper which is his licence and says to him or her, 'Receive the cure of souls which is both yours and mine.'

The suggestion is that the vicar and bishop are in this together, though it often does not feel like it for the vicar. It is possible that the vicar will not see the bishop again for several years. It is likely that the vicar will never discuss with the bishop what is going on in the parish.

Support and supervision

The vicar will not be totally alone. There will be neighbouring clergy in the chapter. There will be an archdeacon whom the vicar is likely to meet, or at least see, once a year at a big service called the Archdeacon's Visitation, and maybe on other occasions. The vicar is also likely to have a ministry review once every two or three years in which there is an opportunity to talk with an archdeacon or another member of the diocesan staff about how things are going in their work. There is also probably a crisis hotline, someone in the diocese with whom a vicar can speak for advice on dealing with a difficult pastoral matter or to talk through a personal crisis. Many vicars' marital breakdowns have been repaired through such a service and nervous breakdowns have been averted. It is good for clergy to know these are there, even if they don't use them.

What does not exist for vicars is anything remotely resembling supervision. No counselling organisation operates without its staff having regular meetings with their own supervisor to work through matters that their work raises for them. No business operates successfully without a clear line-management structure. No large organisation is without its human resources or personnel specialists. Vicars have none of these.

An irony about the situation is that the word 'bishop' actually means a supervisor. Supervisor is simply the word from Latin roots which is equivalent to the Greek *episcopos*, from which the English 'bishop' derives. But bishops do not supervise in any sense similar to current English usage. They can't. They don't have the time. They have too many other demands. They have national responsibilities within the Church of England. People are looking to them for guidance and vision. And they have too many clergy in their dioceses. A hundred and fifty vicars is a small diocese. Three hundred is not unusual.[4]

But neither do some of the bishops have much experience of being a vicar. A third of the diocesan bishops have none. They did a curacy, then worked as a chaplain, or taught in a college or university, or had a diocesan post. They were noticed, considered suitable, and made a bishop. On average the diocesan bishops in post in 2004 had spent seven years as a vicar.[5]

So the bishops may be doing their job well but the vicars cannot rely on them to know what is going on in their parishes or to know what it is like being a vicar. Perhaps the archdeacon has some idea. Maybe the vicars in neighbouring parishes know what is happening if the chapter is working well. But it is possible for vicars to feel very isolated. It is also possible for them to lose track of what they are trying to do, to get overstressed by the demands of other people or their own expectations, to feel they have to keep up a good front and that they can't voice their disappointments anywhere, and to retreat for survival. The retreat may take various forms, ranging from alcohol abuse to simply doing the minimum to get by. Others take time out and recharge.

There are a lot of retreat houses and support organisations across the country. Some work quietly. Some have a high profile. In 2002 The Society of Mary and Martha in Devon published a document called *Affirmation and Accountability*[6] as a result of its own work and a wide consultation with people working within the church. This identifies many of the symptoms and causes of malaise among the parish clergy. It also makes recommendations. Its subtitle is 'Practical suggestions for preventing clergy stress, sickness and ill-health retirement'. Whilst these suggestions do not require a radical restructuring of the church, dioceses are realising that taking these suggestions on board will still take time, money and dedication. And it will require some change. This is both inevitable and difficult in the Church of England.

The authors of *Affirmation and Accountability* say that they meet many clergy who do not know what they are 'for'. This is one serious cause of stress among clergy because, as the report says, 'without this anchoring central knowledge they are prey to a host of inappropriate expectations, fed further by their own anxiety'.[7] A vicar can sit and watch the television and envy the doctors, vets and detectives of the TV dramas. All these people know what they are for and can tell when they have done the job. Doctors make people well, vets make animals well and detectives solve crimes. Builders repair and put up houses and teachers help children understand things and develop skills. They can know what they are aiming for and know when they have done it. At least that is how it can seem from the outside. But for the clergy often the aim can be unclear and the work never finished.

Some clergy, however, do have a clear idea of what they are 'for'. They are there to help people grow in faith, or to build community, or bring spiritual healing, or help people worship and pray. A difficulty then can be knowing how this fits in with the whole life of the church and with all the other things which they seem to be expected to do, many of which seem to have very little connection with this task for which they thought they were ordained. The problem in this case is not that the vicar doesn't have a clear idea of what his or her job should be but that other people don't, or that they have a different idea. Parishioners, PCC members, churchwardens and diocesan officers might have quite different ideas of what the vicar should be doing. This too can be a serious cause of frustration and stress.

If the clergy are to be able to work in an effective and healthy way in the future what is needed is a clear picture of the parish clergy's role. Not only the clergy need this but other people do as well. Developing a clear picture of what the clergy are for and their role in the church is not just a task for the clergy but for all church members.

History

Archdeacon Richard Cutter arrived early at Pickton Magna. He had left plenty of time for the journey and thought he might call in on Angela Watson at Pusham or Peter Fynn at Great Barwood. He hadn't seen Angela since the visitation in May or Peter since his induction, but at both vicarages no one was in.

Pickton Magna had been without a vicar now for ten months and despite his best efforts and an advertisement there was still no one in line to take it on. But that was not the reason for this visit. He was here to inspect some stonework. The architect had expressed concern in his quinquennial inspection and the PCC were thinking they might have to replace two pinnacles on the tower. He was here to have a look and advise on a way forward and was waiting for Tom Adams, one of the churchwardens. But he wasn't going up the tower till Tom arrived, so he looked around the church.

Bright and new beside the tower arch was a framed list of all the rectors and vicars of the parish. It began with a rector called John in 1346 – just in time for the Black Death, thought Richard. The next rector was in 1382. Maybe John lived on a long time. Perhaps he succumbed to the plague and the parish was without a priest for a generation. There was no knowing.

Five more rectors were listed: men who would have farmed their glebe and collected their tithes from the parishioners, maintained the building and supported the poor with the income.

Then the list changed to vicars in 1462. Perhaps the living passed to an abbey who appointed their vicar. He did not know but it might be in the records somewhere.

In 1540 Thomas Pawlett became the vicar and appeared to

remain so until 1561. That was an exciting time to be a parish priest. Edward I and his reforms and the Book of Common Prayer. English instead of Latin. Then Mary turning it all back to Rome, and Elizabeth making the church Protestant again. How did men like Thomas Pawlett survive? Perhaps they were better off in a place like Pickton Magna where no one in authority bothered you much.

James Whitborne was not so lucky. Appointed vicar in 1639, he was obviously removed by the Puritans after the Civil War and replaced by Richard Rogers, their own man, who was in turn removed in 1660 and James Whitborne returned.

The Archdeacon wondered how many of those listed in the eighteenth century actually lived in Pickton, or even came here. One of his predecessors had looked at his archdeacon's visitation reports for the period and found that in the whole archdeaconry, where there were now a hundred and fifty parishes, there had been only sixteen resident clergy in 1742, and half of them had lived in Dorminster so their sons could attend the grammar school.

All those listed in the eighteen hundreds would have lived here, most of the time. Not that there were many of them. James Pontleford did forty-two years and George Pontleford another thirty-seven. Perhaps he was his son, but probably his grandson, with the patronage held in the family.

Pickton continued to have a vicar right through to the present time. There was a drive in the late nineteenth century to have a gentleman vicar in every parish, but when the number reached its peak still a fifth of parishes were without one. Many of those would have been in the industrial city centres, but still a lot of country parishes would also have been without.

But most had a vicar, and that is what is remembered. It became the norm and is still within living memory, and he, the Archdeacon of Trent, like most archdeacons and country clergy, are dealing with that expectation every day. People still talk as if every parish should have a vicar and this clustering of parishes was some kind of aberration.

The linking of Pickton Parva does not feature on the Pickton table of incumbents. Anyone looking at it might think that Gordon Black, the most recent vicar, was just the vicar of this one parish. In the same way they might think that those vicars back before the nineteenth century only had one parish and not realise that many of them would have had several others as well. But theirs might have been in different parts of the country, providing an income for a man who might have lived anywhere.

Gordon Black's name was at the end of the list. Seven hundred years and fifty vicars. The list had been written out by a skilled calligrapher and illuminated like a medieval manuscript. It was beautifully done. But there was no room on the list for any more. The list went right down to the bottom of the frame.

Richard remembered authorising this list when the PCC wanted to put it into the church a year or so ago when Gordon had said he was retiring. He hadn't realised that it was designed without a space for any more vicars. He hadn't thought to check.

But then he heard footsteps on the path and the church door opened. Tom Adams came in.

'Morning Archdeacon. Sorry to keep you waiting.' Tom was a local dairy farmer and had been churchwarden for a number of years.

'I see you've given up trying to get a new vicar, then,' said the Archdeacon.

'What do you mean?' he said.

'Your list of vicars. There's no room for another one.'

Tom thought for a moment.

'Ah, that's 'cos we bought two frames while we were at it. The new vicar will be the start of a new list.'

4

The Myth of the Country Parson

The word 'parson' is derived from the same word as 'person'. In the Middle Ages the French legal term 'parsone' was applied to the person who was taken to be responsible for the Church's, or God's, property in a parish. They were the person who could be sued if something went terribly wrong. In time in England the word came to refer to the rector of a parish, the person entitled to the tithes. Then it came to apply to the church minister responsible for the parish whether he was a rector or a vicar. Later the word 'parson' came to be applied to whichever ordained minister lived in the parish: the rector, the vicar or the curate. They were the church person. They personified the church. If they took an interest in something it was seen as the church taking an interest. If the parson failed to attend or to visit the church was not interested.

The word is rarely used now but the idea of the parson lingers. There are still people who only feel they have been visited by the church when the vicar has called, regardless of the number of times other church members have called on them. People say about how the church ought to be involved in local affairs and mean by that that the vicar ought to take an interest. It might be that the chairman of the parish council, the local district councillor, the chair of the NFU and the president of the local WI are all regular worshippers at the parish church but it is the vicar attending meetings which is seen as the church taking an interest. At the same time it is often said that the church should not be involved in politics, by which people usually mean the clergy. The local MP may be regularly in church and on the parish's electoral roll, but that is not the same thing. The clergy are still often seen as the church.

A model of ministry

In the many books that were written to encourage and guide young clergy in the nineteenth century the most quoted and referred-to figure was George Herbert, an aristocrat of the seventeenth century who gave up the life of a diplomat and courtier to become the vicar of the parish of Bemerton in Wiltshire, and who wrote a book about what he was trying to achieve. Herbert's poetry is generally better known, particularly as some of his poems were subsequently turned into hymns, but his book, *A Priest to the Temple, or the Country Parson*, has possibly been just as influential within the church.[1] Few read the book now but his ideas continue to be influential.

According to Herbert the country parson was to live in his parish and become acquainted with its ways. He was to visit and know his parishioners, taking an interest in their affairs, and not standing aloof from their concerns. The country parson 'upon the afternoons in the weekdays, takes occasion sometimes to visit in person, now one quarter of his parish now another'.[2] He was to pray for his parishioners and look after them. 'If there is any of his flock sick he is their physician, or at least his wife.'[3] The country parson would grow herbs and simples so that he could make remedies for his sick parishioners and was to study the Scriptures diligently so that he might have remedies for their spiritual ills. He was to teach them the catechism and encourage them to pray and worship God Sunday by Sunday and through the year. The country parson was to ensure that everyone in the parish had work, that none were idle or needed to beg. He was not to be severe, though firm when necessary, nor to favour the rich against the poor, but was to have a ready sense of humour and be able to enjoy the simple pleasures of country life. He would be a shepherd who knew his flock and who was known by them.

Herbert did not invent the idea of the country parson. Among Chaucer's companions on the pilgrimage to Canterbury was a parson, rich in holy thought and work, a learned man who would truly preach Christ's gospel and devoutly teach his parishioners; benign, diligent and patient in adversity. He was reluctant to exert pressure for his tithes but would willingly give to those in need and would visit on foot those of his parish who were ill or in trouble, regardless of the weather.[4]

Herbert's short book turns this image into a model of ministry in two senses of the word. It can provide a theoretical model for the country vicar: a way of thinking about the vicar's life, attitudes and work that is succinct and holds together the different possibilities. It is simple. He put it this way, 'Christ being not to continue on earth, but after he had fulfilled the work of reconciliation, to be received up into heaven, he constituted deputies in his place, and these are priests.'[5] 'The country parson desires to be all to his parish.'[6] The parish priest is Christ's deputy and must be and do everything that is necessary for the welfare of the parishioners.

Herbert provides a model in another sense as well, in the sense of an ideal. He wrote his book for himself. It was not published till nineteen years after his death. It was, for him, 'a mark to aim at'.[7] It was what he was going to try to do. We do not know the extent to which he succeeded. No doubt he would not have said he had done so. His poetry is full of references to the love of God, to God's grace and forgiveness. It does not suggest that Herbert had any sense of being successful and achieving his aim, although his parishioners may well have thought so. But however close he got to the standard he had set himself he did not maintain his ministry for very long. He died three years after beginning his parish ministry.

But Herbert's picture is powerful and lives on. Many who have never heard of George Herbert are familiar with this image of the Country Parson, which will be there among their own ideas of what country vicars are about. In 1993 Anthony

Russell, Bishop of Ely, concluded a trilogy of books on the rural church with a study of Herbert's ideas, commending them to the church for serious consideration at the end of the twentieth century.[8] Herbert's parson was a priest, pastor, teacher and shepherd, and though the situation of the present-day country vicar is very different, says Russell, these should be his principal roles. Herbert's image is the one that the country vicar should have before him. In 2003 the writer and Reader Ronald Blythe produced a new edition of Herbert's book, again as a serious recommendation for the Church of England in the present time.[9]

The 2003 BBC documentary *A Country Parish* presents the vicar Jamie Allen as attempting to work to this model. Although the title suggested it was about the parish, the programmes were about the vicar and showed him taking services, visiting the bereaved, providing support for the lady who had lost her dog, working with children in the school, conducting the funeral of a much loved parishioner. He is seen out raising money for the church and surveying the damage to one of the church buildings. He meets with his churchwardens but there is no footage of what they actually do. They appear as avuncular figures giving moral support to their vicar who is doing the church's work. A team of flower arrangers prepares one of the churches for a Christmas flower festival, and they do it for him, their new young vicar. And when the harvest festival service is fixed on the same day as the countryside march it is the vicar's fault, as if no one else had any responsibility for pointing out to him at an early stage that there was a clash of dates.

It may be that Jamie Allen was not working to that model of ministry at all. It may be that the producers by their editing presented him in that way because that is what they wanted to show or what they thought viewers wanted to see. It may also have been that parishioners wanted to see Jamie in that way. Jamie himself may have had a very different idea in his mind of what he was about, but that did not come through in the programmes. What came through was what many people expect to see in a country vicar, that they are the church personified, doing and being everything that the church ought to do and be.

Ideals from the past

George Herbert was the vicar of an agricultural village of two hundred people who all worked within the parish. They did not read, they had no newspapers, TV or radio. They did not vote, and if they travelled they went on foot except one or two wealthy people, like Herbert himself, who would have ridden or driven a carriage. Their food was grown locally or purchased in Salisbury market two miles away. They would all have been Christians and all have been considered members of the Church of England who worshipped according to the *Book of Common Prayer*. Yet Herbert's picture of the Country Parson remains the principal idea and expectation of many people living in the country and the model that many clergy have in their minds. The parson idea is still often thought to provide a working image for a vicar responding to the needs of the several thousand people in several parishes and assisting the churches in their task. Despite all the differences between Herbert's culture and present-day England and all the changes in the organisation of the Church of England, the country vicar is still often expected to operate as a fourteenth-, seventeenth- or nineteenth-century country parson.

One reason for this is simply that the Country Parson is a clear image. It is not a job description or a list of aims and objectives. Herbert himself writes of what the Country Parson 'will do'. He holds before his readers an imaginary person doing these various tasks. This is concrete, and imaginable, and not simply abstract. It also comes with the weight of Herbert's own personality and example as a man who gave up a great deal to follow his vocation, and who was known himself for his depth of prayer and concern for his parishioners.

Another reason is that George Herbert is a familiar figure. He is a part of the great English religious tradition. His name ranks with those of John Keble and John Newton, Thomas Cranmer and William Tyndale. His poems appear in hymnbooks and have a poetical beauty that will hold them alongside the *Book of Common Prayer*.

George Herbert's idea of the Country Parson also has some important strengths which many people recognise and do not want to see lost from the ministry of the rural church. The country parson is rooted in a place. At best the parson is a local theologian, attempting to relate the gospel to the realities and complexities of life in a particular location, not simply concerned with generalities. It is possible for theological thinking to move solely in the realms of abstraction rather than engage with the mundane matters of rural life.

The parson's ministry is to people in their individuality and to the communities of which they are part. Contrary to much modern culture, it is increasingly recognised by many psychotherapists that people cannot be treated as isolated individuals but as part of a matrix of relationships. The country parson is concerned not only with the individual's relationship with God but with the spiritual health of communities.

For Herbert's parson his life as well as his ministry is grounded in prayer and the worship of God. The work stems from the minister's own relationship with and vision of God rather than from second-hand theories. It includes study of the Bible, not simply drawing on personal feelings and ideas but aiming to hear and engage with the Word of God.

The parson is also concerned about the physical needs of his parishioners. More clergy today are likely to be engaging with the local health authority or social services than brewing up medicines in their kitchens, though some country clergy in the early twentieth century still did just that. Herbert's parson with his cures and simples is a reminder of Jesus' concern for the physical well-being of people and not just their souls.

In the myth

Another reason for the persistence of the Country Parson model of ministry is that it fits in neatly and nicely with the greater myth of Rural England. It is a part of that much bigger picture which holds together ideas of church and community, history and landscape: an image which affects not only how people think about rural England but how they feel about it, what they want from it, what they will look for, what they will campaign for, and even, perhaps, what they will die for.

In the middle of that imaginary England of villages where people know their neighbours and look out for each other, where they watch cricket on the green in the summer sunshine and drink pints of beer outside the pub, where the children play in the meadows and woods and where elderly ladies walk to evensong, there is the vicar, the parson, saying his prayers in the church, writing letters and preparing sermons in his study in the morning and out visiting in the afternoon. The Country Parson moves gracefully from seventeenth-century Wiltshire to the neverland of English mythology. Maybe he now has a bicycle rather than a horse and carriage, but he is the same man, of a piece with the image which sells loaves of wholemeal bread, shelves of books and racks of calendars, and draws people from towns and cities to holidays or retirement in the English countryside.

This idea of a rural society is in such stark contrast to the lives that so many people in England actually lead that they want to escape into it, which they do in costume dramas on television, in novels from Agatha Christie to Miss Read, and possibly, by going to church. This rural dream is another world, which may say important things about how life could, or should, be but it is not life as it is lived. It is not rural England as it really is now. There is much about rural life, at least in many areas, which people continue to find attractive. The current movement of population from the cities to the countryside is not balanced by a flow of disappointed people moving the other way. The smaller flow from the country to the towns and cities is generally people who have grown up in the areas and have to move away to find work or affordable housing or people moving to where medical services, shops and public transport are better.

But the countryside is not an idyll. Some of what people

look for can be found there: less traffic, less noise and lower crime rates, more open space, fields, trees, skies in which the stars can be seen at night and seasons which are noticeable in the landscape. There are usually footpaths, in some places there are grassy riverbanks, and sometimes the local buildings blend well with the landscape, built of the local stone and well weathered. Neighbours will often say hello or at least make eye contact and over a short period of time one can come to recognise, if not actually know, many of the people who live nearby.

Some of these neighbours are not easy to get on with. Others might be extremely difficult. A village might not be a small happy community. Many small communities are divided between incomers and those who have lived there a long time. Others have feuds going back generations. The roads have less traffic but are often more dangerous, being narrow and often without footpaths. There is crime committed both by local people and others who come out from cities targeting the more affluent rural areas. Children are not safe from potential abuse or young people from drugs. Public transport is poorer partly because the population is more thinly spread but also because it is less subsidised in rural areas than in the cities.[10] People often have to travel into the cities to visit big shops or major hospitals. At times the roads will be muddy and the air smell of manure or livestock.

In short the situation is that most people who move to the countryside want to stay there unless their circumstances change as a result of age or illness. Some people soon realise that an isolated location has too many drawbacks and move, if they are able to, into a big village or small town. But no one who lives in the countryside thinks it is an idyllic existence. The result of this is that the myth is adjusted so that the countryside is thought of as having slowly declined from the good old days when people did not move around so much and everyone knew each other, before the traffic and the big tractors, and when things were much more leisurely and everyone lived closer to the soil. This is not a new idea. The cultural historian Raymond Williams points out how time and again in English writing authors set their novels and poems in an earlier era when the countryside was supposedly something closer to their ideal.[11] It is as if they are aware that the countryside as they now experience it is not what it ought to be but believe that it was something closer to that in the past. And so part of the myth of the countryside is that it has a history of slow decline from a life of creative work, simple pleasures, supportive community, health and stability.

Other stories

Rural England certainly has a history and that story can be told in many ways. For a start it is a story of mobility. There is a widespread idea that life in English villages was very settled in the past and that only recently have there been movements of population. This is not actually the case. There has always been movement. Rowland Parker in *The Common Stream*, his study of one community over several centuries, pointed out that it was very unusual for a surname in a village to last more than three generations, even three centuries ago.[12] And amongst the people in a rural area today who consider themselves as belonging to the place and having always lived there, a little bit of research, whether in church registers or a conversation in the pub, often reveals that the family moved in within the last hundred years: certainly long enough for the current generation to have grown up there but not so long that they were around even during the nineteenth century. There are exceptions to this, but they are usually amongst the families that owned land.

There certainly was less movement in the past than there is in many places now. Two centuries ago the desperately poor could not move. They were dependent on the parish for support. But those with trades and those who were fit could move and often did. The story of rural England is better told as one of a slow movement of many people from place to place; a movement which has accelerated in recent decades as the countryside has become a desirable place to live and the development of motorways and fast trains has enabled many more people who work in cities to live in the country. But the countryside never was a place where people stayed and nothing much changed.

The story of the countryside can also be told as one of dispossession. At the time that George Herbert was writing the enclosures were beginning to take off. Slowly, in parish after parish, open fields and people's common lands were being divided up amongst a few in the community, fenced or hedged off with hawthorn, and made into farms. Productivity went up but for most people food became something they struggled to buy, not something they could grow for themselves. A surfeit of labour often led to lower wages even when the price of food was going up. The organisation of workers' unions was prohibited and, even when the right to strike was won, migrations to the cities continued as people tried to escape the continuing desperate poverty of the countryside. That movement continues now as many local people who grew up in the countryside are unable to afford homes there or the cost of transport, and move to the towns or cities. The influx of more wealthy people who want a home in the country increases the price of property and pushes it beyond the reach of the people who have grown up in the villages but earn low wages. An increase in the number of wealthier people who can afford to run several cars in the family reduces the demand for public transport on which the lower-paid sometimes depend.

The story of rural England can also be told as one of technological change. The enclosures were part of a movement for improved agriculture which in time saw the development of seed drills and reapers, of threshing machines and binders, of tractors and milking machines, combines, herbicides, pesticides and computerised records. It is a process which has continued from Herbert's day to our own, and all along the line there has been a slow reduction in employment opportunities for people in the countryside. There were reactions against this in the eighteenth century as the changes began to have a serious effect. Luddites broke up machinery and mobs burnt ricks and barns in protest, but the mechanisation was not stopped. Schools that closed in the 1960s because they were no longer viable had been full at the turn of the century, largely with the children of labourers.

Technological development has also vastly improved the lives of rural people that remained. Electricity reached the rural areas after the cities and together with improvements in building techniques led to warmer, drier homes. The pretty country cottages of today are the ones that have survived from earlier centuries. Much of the worst housing has been demolished, left to collapse or almost totally rebuilt. In the last four decades the telephone and terrestrial and later satellite television have incorporated the culture of rural England into that of the whole of Western society. Children in the countryside now watch exactly the same TV programmes, play the same computer games and listen to the same music as those in the cities, even in the remotest areas where their nearest friends might live several miles away.

In the nineteenth century many clergy going to work in rural areas were shocked by the living conditions and the social life of the poorer country people. As photography developed this shock was then felt by many more middle-class people in the cities who had romantic notions about the countryside but now saw realistic pictures. Some Victorian clergy referred to the part of the village to which they rarely went as 'the dark village'. It was often characterised by domestic violence and alcohol abuse. Many local history societies today are amused to find how many pubs there once were in their village, but these were not snug cottages decorated with horse brasses where the locals could quietly play dominoes. These were places selling cheap beer or cider which could enable people to find some escape from the drudgery of their working lives.

The story of rural England can also be told as one of environmental damage, from the time when the great forests were cleared on to the Middle Ages when vast flocks of sheep, often owned by monasteries, overgrazed hillsides; then later when the commons were hedged and the habitats of so many birds and animals were destroyed and then, later still, many of those hedges were removed, destroying still more habitats and causing serious soil erosion. Canals, railways, mines, quarries and roads have all changed the shape of the land, factories and mills have polluted it and the expansion of towns, cities and suburbs has reduced the area of the countryside. Pesticides have destroyed food chains for wildlife and now genetically modified crops could lead to irreversible alterations to existing plant life.

Or the story can be told as one of exploitation. For many years the wages and conditions of agricultural workers were among the worst in the country. Even after the right had been won to form unions and take industrial action it was still often very difficult in rural communities to act, when the unit of employment was relatively small, when the worker lived in a house tied to the job, when his low wages were sweetened by payments in kind which could be stopped at the farmer's whim and when the local magistrate was possibly the farmer or the farmer's friend. In the nineteenth century and into the twentieth farmers were powerful people in the countryside. Folksongs would tell the happy tale of a poor lad who was taken in by a generous farmer and came to marry the farmer's daughter. This was the stuff that dreams were made of for most people in the English countryside. The reality was continued hardship or migration to the city where things might be a little better.

The other major employers in nineteenth-century rural England were the big estates. There was work at the big house for unmarried girls who would go into service, for stable boys and garden hands. A few might stay on as part of the domestic staff or as gardeners and grooms. Others would have to move on. Some of the wealthy families looked after their staff well. Others did not, and some of the tales passed on in families are of exploitation and abuse. There are many country people who look back to their time as farm workers or growing up in tied cottages as something they would not want to repeat. Even now the wages of agricultural workers are not high. In tourism wages are notoriously low and there is poor job security. There are many people in the more scenic rural areas who have wages in the summer and benefit in the winter.

The story of rural England is not a descent from peace and contentment. The peaceful contented society of so many English dreams never existed. The countryside has always been a theatre of social conflict as well as of community life, of discontent, poverty and grief, as well as beauty and celebration. There has always been movement, migration and change, injustice and unsung heroism.

In all this change and development the church has had a part. Many of the early developments in English agriculture were carried out by the monasteries, from the draining of the Somerset wetlands to the grazing of great flocks on the Cotswolds. Later, during the enclosures and during the riots and strikes, the local parson was often involved, standing beside the farmer and landowner. There were country parsons who stood up for those who were losing their access to land through the enclosure movement or who suffered very low wages. But there were many who did not. Some tried to act as mediators, as the Vicar of Tolpuddle did, unsuccessfully, before the local farm workers went on strike. The clergy came largely from the same social class as the farmers and smaller landowners. Others were from the commercial classes. None came from among the agricultural workers or the other rural poor. For many Anglican clergy one's station or position in life was something ordained by God. Stability was part of the way that things were meant to be. Even the 1922 edition of the popular *Hymns Ancient and Modern* included in the hymn 'All things bright and beautiful' the verse:

> The rich man in his castle,
> The poor man at his gate,
> God made them, high or lowly,
> And ordered their estate.[13]

The Vicar of Bednall in Staffordshire in the 1920s would hit with his horsewhip boys who failed to lift their caps as he drove past in his carriage.

Other ministers

Down the centuries many country vicars have been devoted parsons, beavering away in their parishes with little or no recognition from the church hierarchy. Others have seen their office as a means to a modest income and a life of leisure. Some have rarely set foot in their parishes, and others would not have done so if the law had not been changed to make them. Being human and being people of their time and culture, they have been very different in their attitudes and in their lives.

But the ministers of the church down the centuries have not only been the parsons. Within the Church of England every parish has had churchwardens since the Middle Ages. They have represented the church. They have at times had responsibility for administering the local provision for the destitute and the poor. They have looked after church buildings and churchyards. Parishes have also often had a clerk, whose duty at times was to read the services if there was no vicar to do it. There have been sextons who looked after the churchyard and rang the bell and vergers who prepared the church for worship. There have also been other church members who have supported their neighbours, mediated in disputes, laid out the dead and prepared them for burial, nursed the sick, comforted mourners and prayed for their fellow parishioners.

But the church has also had people with an itinerant ministry. Since its separation from the Roman Church in the Tudor period the Church of England has had little place for itinerant ministers. It was designed or developed for a stable situation in which people lived in their parishes for most of their lives and worshipped round the year from Advent to All Saints' Day. Before the Reformation there had been itinerant preachers: friars and Lollards moving from place to place to proclaim the gospel and counter heresy. George Herbert's contemporary George Fox travelled from place to place in the beginning of what came to be called the Quaker movement. Others in the independent churches moved around, either to spread the word or to avoid persecution. In the eighteenth century John Wesley and the early Methodists refused to be tied to one place but went where they saw a need, which was often among people who were alienated from their local parish church. In the various waves of evangelical revival there have been itinerant preachers travelling from parish to parish, to the frustration or delight of the local vicar. Roman Catholic priests also moved from place to place, particularly during the centuries when the Roman Church was suppressed.

There have also been radical communities. The monasteries of England were dissolved just before the Church of England took on a Protestant theology which allowed little space for a monastic life, but there were still people who saw the nature of Christian discipleship as demanding a community life different from simple residence within an English parish. George Herbert's friend Nicholas Ferrar established a community at Little Gidding to try to live out the Christian gospel in a shared common life.

In the independent churches, especially the Congregationalists and Baptists, there was a strong sense that the church was not an institution within the fabric of social life but was a gathering of disciples of Christ. They might have a minister or pastor which the congregation had chosen and appointed to teach and support them in their Christian lives. This person might be helped financially by the congregation. Often the minister would support himself and his family with other work, and would see his task in the church as helping the local congregation in their own Christian ministries.

What the Church of England needs now is a way of thinking about the work of the country vicar which is realistic. It needs to be realistic in the sense that it is suited to the life of the rural church and rural society as it actually is and not to rural society and the church as they were a century ago or as they are in a rural fantasy. But it also needs to be realistic in the sense of being manageable by clergy who do not have infinite resources of energy and time and who need to have more to their lives than their parish work. There was much about the country parson model which was valuable and it would be good to be able to keep that. But developing an appropriate model for the present time and the future needs to begin not with a model from a very different society but with some fundamental thinking of what the church is, what it does and what it is for.

The Move

'Vernon Semper will have to move,' said the Archdeacon of Trent. 'One of his wardens spoke to me and was very concerned so I went to see him. He can't cope. He's getting up at five in the morning, working till late, and exhausted.'

'Vernon Semper?' said the bishop. 'What does he look like?'

'Small. Dark crinkly hair, thinning. Glasses. Quietly spoken. Grey shirt and tweed jacket.'

'Oh, yes,' said the bishop. 'Lovely man. Where is he now?'

'Bladeney, with Lepsham, Ragdon and Rotton Mupney. He's had the four parishes for three years now.'

'Oh yes. I remember.'

'Yes, he'd been at Bladeney for twelve years and we needed to form a bigger grouping. So when Bernard Madison retired we put the two pairs of parishes together to make a four-parish benefice – Bladeney and Lepsham with Ragdon and Rotton Mupney. The problem is that in his first twelve years Vernon developed a particular way of doing things. He was the classic old-style country vicar. Lots of visiting, school assemblies, took all the services himself, ran a small village choir. That sort of thing. They loved him. He was everyone's uncle.

'But Bladeney and Lepsham together only had a population of eight hundred. Ragdon is much bigger. It's got the Handfield housing development. There are over a thousand houses there now, and it's still growing. With twice as many churches and four times as many people he just can't operate the same way, but he's trying to.'

'So what do you suggest?' asked the bishop. 'Can we put in some support to help him through?'

79

'We can't afford to put in another stipendiary and that would defeat the whole object of joining the four parishes together. And I think it's too late for any kind of training. He would need to come at things a completely different way and I don't think he can do that. I think we've got to move him out so he can leave with honour. He won't have to resign and he might avoid a breakdown.'

'And his family? Is he married?'

'Yes. His children are grown up. His wife is seriously asthmatic and depressive, and the stress on her husband isn't helping her. She doesn't drive and there are no buses in Bladeney.'

'So where do you suggest he moves to?'

'We could offer him priest-in-charge of Wellham, to help them through their crisis.'

'Where their previous vicar joined that housechurch and took half the congregation away with him?'

'Yes. I think he'd be a good person to help them through that. Lots of TLC for them and a simple two-church set-up for him. His wife would have to leave her friends in Bladeney but at least she'd have shops and a bus service.'

'That sounds good. Would he go? If he's been in Bladeney fifteen years he must be pretty settled.'

'I think he'd go if it came from you and he could see it as a positive move rather than bailing out.'

'OK then,' said the bishop. 'Put it that way. Tell him I really want him to help us out with a serious pastoral problem. In Wellham.'

'And then we look for someone else for Bladeney. Someone who can come in fresh but live with the ghost of Uncle Vernon. I can hear them now. "He doesn't visit like Vernon used to."'

5

The Three-dimensional Church

The Church in England

One difficulty with thinking about the church is that the word 'church' is rather slippery. It can mean a number of different things. Clearly for many people the word means 'the clergy', as in the question often put to vicars over sausage rolls after a funeral, 'When did you go into the church?' It is easy for a vicar to be facetious and say 'When I was baptised', or 'Just before the funeral', but every vicar knows that the person means 'When were you ordained?'

But the base meaning of the word 'church' is not the clergy. When St Paul wrote his letters to the churches in Philippi, Rome and Corinth he was not writing to clergy but to a group of Christians. The English word 'church' is used to translate the Greek word *ecclesia*, which Paul actually used, and for him it meant the people of God. It was not a term invented by Christians but Paul would have known it from his childhood when he studied the Jewish Scriptures in Greek and found it as the term for a gathering of the Hebrew people. In his later writings he used it of the people who had come to see Jesus as the Messiah or, in Greek, the Christ, whether or not they were also Jews. When Paul's writings and other Christian Scriptures were first translated into English either the word 'congregation' or the word 'church' was used. It was 'church' that stuck.

So it is that one can refer to the world church, meaning all the people across the world who are Christians. Or one can talk about the local church, meaning the Christians in a particular place. And in the church's services as well as the Bible this is what the word refers to. Not the clergy but all the Christian people. However it is easy to see how the idea of the church as the clergy slipped into general thinking. In a society like that of George Herbert when everyone was reckoned as a Christian then the church in its principal meaning simply meant everyone. So why not say 'everyone'? But there were people who represented the church, who were the church person in the place, so they, the parsons, became 'the church'.

Or the building became 'the church': the building with its lectern and communion table, and later its organ and pews, which was used for church services. So in a society in which everyone was a part of the church, in its first meaning, any religious distinctions were not between those who were church and those who were not, as they were for St Paul, but between those who had 'gone into the church', meaning the clergy, and those who had not, meaning everyone else. Or the distinction was between those who 'went to church', meaning they attended church services, and those who didn't. And at times those who didn't could be punished.

But then, different denominations formed or appeared in rural England. Presbyterian, Congregationalist, Baptist and Methodist churches formed and the Roman Catholic Church was allowed to come out of hiding. So for many people 'the Church' meant the Church of England. Others were distinguished by their full title or referred to as 'Chapel'.

For some time members of the Church of England thought of themselves as the proper church whilst other denominations were some kind of aberration. Rural folk history has plenty of tales of Methodists and Congregationalists being ignored by Anglican clergy. And there are plenty of ministers of other churches who will tell of how in the very recent past there have been Church of England vicars who always assumed that they were going to be the chairman of any local inter-church meeting.

Belonging to the Church of England

The Church of England has a very open membership policy which can give a refuge or even a welcome to people who are in a very exploratory state in their faith. One can sign up on the local Church of England Electoral Roll without having to answer any questions about what you believe, how often you will go to church, how much you will contribute to the costs of running the church or about how you live. All you need is to have been baptised and declare yourself a member of the Church of England. And, despite rumours to the contrary, you do not even have to be baptised to be married in a church or have your funeral there. This openness seems very odd to some who expect the church, if it stands for anything, to demand that people signing up as members ascribe to some declaration of belief or make some commitment about their involvement. But it does give an opportunity for people to be members who have a sense that they want to be a part of the church but are not sure of what they believe or of what that part might be. It also gives those who already belong a free-dom to question and think for themselves without fearing that if they move too far in any direction they might be excluded.

However, it does mean that the Church of England has very fuzzy boundaries. When St Paul wrote to the Church in Corinth it was known to everyone in the congregation who was and who was not a part of the church. And when George Herbert wrote *The Country Parson* it was also clear. The church in Bemerton was everyone. Now the boundary is not at all clear for the local branch of the Church of England. Some people obviously are members. Some clearly are not and would be offended if it were suggested they were. But many people like to think of themselves as members, or would not like to think they were not members, or want to be considered members but do not want to be expected to actually do any-thing much as far as the church organisation and worship is concerned.

There are people who want to draw the boundaries quite

83

clearly. They perhaps believe they are selling people short by suggesting that being an adult Christian is simply a matter of having been baptised as a baby and now signing an Electoral Roll form. They might think they are selling the church short by allowing people to carry on considering themselves members of the church when they do nothing for its corporate life and contribute nothing to pay its quite considerable bills. However, it is also the case that great upset can be caused in country churches by drawing lines and boundaries when it comes to the church's services. Refusing to baptise children whose parents do not come regularly to the church or appearing to put obstacles in the way of couples wanting weddings can cause, at the very least, disappointment and antagonism within the community, and in a small parish that can take a long time to sort out. The parish is not like a small office or factory where the boss can get everyone together and talk things through, explain where he is coming from and deal individually with misunderstandings or offence. In a country parish a thousand conversations can go on about what the vicar has or has not done and the vicar is not able to correct misinformation or explain why he or she has acted in a particular way.

Nevertheless, to try to develop a way of thinking about what country vicars can expect and be expected to do it is necessary to think first about what the church does. The church comes first. A vicar does not make a church and there can be a local church without a vicar. In fact there are many local churches without vicars now as there often have been in the past. A vicar leaves and it might be a year or more before another comes. During that time the church does not disappear or cease to function. The local church carries on with its life, doing the things that churches do. There is often a sense of relief when a new vicar arrives but that is because someone has come to join them who will take responsibility for many of the things they have had to do or organise and who will hopefully be a person with ideas, imagination, understanding, pastoral skills, and much more to bring to their church life.

Community life

Thinking about what the church does is not the same as thinking about everything that goes on in a community, nor what
the vicar gets up to. It is the local church that we are considering and that means we are talking about a particular group
of people within a community. It is not everyone, unless it is
a very exceptional parish, and not just the vicar. That means
thinking of the church as having members and therefore of
the parish as having some residents who are not members.
That does not mean we have to set out who is a member and
who is not; who qualifies and who is counted out. We are
simply thinking about a church as a group of people within a
locality. They are part of a wider community, or even of several communities in which they live and work as well as
extended networks of friends and relations. They are also part
of a wider church, both a national body called the Church of
England and an international network of Christians of many
different denominations and traditions. Our focus is the
church as a loosely bounded group of people, of which the
vicar is one member with particular roles and responsibilities.

In his book *The Isaiah Vision* Raymond Fung, who had
worked on a World Council of Churches project for many
years, put forward the view that wherever you looked in the
world expanding or developing churches were following a
similar pattern.[1] Their church life was characterised by work
within their community, by worship and by people being
willing to learn more of what was involved in being a
Christian. He based this on considerable research and linked
it with a passage from the book of Isaiah in the Old
Testament. The connection with Isaiah was rather tenuous
but also unnecessary. In the Acts of the Apostles it is said that
the first Christians 'devoted themselves to the apostles'
teaching and fellowship, to the breaking of bread and the
prayers' (Acts 2.42). The same pattern is here: community
engagement, worship and discipleship.

The work of any country parish can be seen in the same
way. Fung's research was on expanding churches but it is

85

hard to imagine any church which does not have these three aspects to its common life, even if they are in a rather rudimentary form. Some churches may not do very much in their particular area although they will all have some kind of community life, even if it is little more than turning up at the same place and time on a Sunday morning, and maybe saying 'Good morning' to each other. Every parish church is also going to have an Annual Meeting and meetings of a Parochial Church Council. Many have a fete or Christmas bazaar, which is supposed to be about raising money but which is often kept going because everyone likes the experience of working together. In some parishes it would be much more cost effective for all the volunteers to chip in £10 each and be done with it, but they don't want to do that. They enjoy doing it. Many country churches have a lot more going on, but even in the most sad and run-down congregation the vicar and churchwardens have to talk to each other sometimes. There is bound to be some kind of community life in a church.

Church members will also have some social connections with others in their parish through village events, local government, jumble sales or visiting neighbours. The community life of a village church may also involve links with other parts of the country, and other countries, be it through one member's holiday, another one's work, a young person's year out from college, or a link with a mission partner or an overseas church. One aspect of a local church is going to be its community life.

Worship and prayer

The church's life will also involve worship. Usually this is a Sunday morning service which some church members take part in, maybe only singing hymns and joining in prayers but often more actively. People read lessons, they play the organ or piano, lead prayers, give out hymnbooks, prepare the church for the service, arrange flowers, ring bells, and put the heating on. This too is a corporate activity, but its primary purpose is the worship of God.

It does not necessarily follow that closing a church building removes the church from a village. In some places where a village church has closed a congregation has continued to gather for worship in a village hall or even a farm kitchen. In that different context worship has sometimes developed into new styles and the different meeting place has helped develop a sense of common life which is much stronger than when Sunday worship was thought of as 'going to church' rather than 'meeting together'.

The church at Dunston in Staffordshire was discovered to have dangerous stonework in the spire. An order was placed on the building to close it until repairs were carried out. The immediate question was whether the repairs should be carried out or whether the church should perhaps be closed. People came from far and wide to attend a public meeting and declare forcefully the need to carry out the repairs and reopen the church, which was not an ancient building nor in the village centre. Some of these people at the meeting had never been seen in the church building. The PCC decided to carry out the repairs and to hold regular services in the village hall until it was done. It took a year or so to get the money together, by the end of which time people said how good it had been worshipping in the village hall. They had sat around the table on chairs and sung to the piano. Then after every service they had coffee together. The whole thing had developed a strong sense of being together in worship rather than simply going to church. They hoped this feeling would not disappear once they were back in the church. Sadly it did, although there are probably many places where that community sense would have remained.

Discipleship

A church's life will also involve some kind of teaching and learning. This might come from the sharing of experiences in ordinary conversation, or from things that the members have done together. It is likely to be expected from the weekly sermon. There may also be a Lent course, or a weekly Bible study, or a group following a course which explores the basics of Christian faith. Then also, of course, people watch television, listen to the radio, and read books. All these can help people think and learn, make connections, imagine new possibilities, or get an idea of how things are for another person and maybe link these up with the traditional teaching of the church or with stories, poems or sayings from the Bible, from hymns or well-known prayers. Learning goes on in all sorts of contexts, some of them deliberately planned like study courses and Sunday Schools, but many of them informal and ad hoc.

The aim of much of the teaching of the church is not simply that people should be able to clarify their ideas about life, the universe and God but that they should be able to live with a deeper or stronger faith. Jesus was known as a teacher but he was not a philosopher or a scientist. His concern was that people should have faith in God and live with love and these will be the aims of much church preaching and teaching. The process of learning and living with Christian faith is often referred to as discipleship: being a disciple of Jesus.

The agenda

It is possible for items on a PCC's agenda to be clustered into these three areas. Doing this can help the members recognise the different aspects of their church life, and encourage them to occasionally reappraise matters which might otherwise go unconsidered for years. Most PCCs will annually consider the fete or the bazaar, which can feature under the heading 'Community'. Having 'Community' as a broad heading can encourage members to think a little more widely, and perhaps bring subjects onto the PCC agenda which might otherwise be left off. Basic questions can be asked. Is this all there is to our community life? Are there other things we should be doing, maybe for people in another part of the world, maybe for our neighbours, or maybe for ourselves?

Many PCCs will review their patterns of worship and their special services from time to time. Even when they don't, someone will occasionally voice a complaint about how 'a number of people are saying they don't like the new services,' or ask, 'Why do we have to sing all these new hymns which we don't know?' Others will come out with ideas, perhaps their own or maybe something that they have heard another parish has done: a Rogation Sunday service, or a procession round the village on Palm Sunday, or a Songs of Praise on a summer's evening. Having a broad heading of 'Worship' on a PCC agenda can encourage thinking about new possibilities beyond the maintenance of present activity, giving space in the meeting for any other matters concerning worship before going on to the next item.

Having a broad heading of 'Discipleship' might raise some questions within people's minds. This is the obvious place to review in a meeting any matters concerning children's work or confirmation, but also adult education as well. In a church which only has Sunday sermons as its diet of adult education the vicar and other preachers might like to know what church members find helpful, and need to know what they do not. But few village churches exist in a vacuum. There may well be someone around who has heard of an Alpha or Emmaus course and wants to ask about it or suggest the church might have one, or there may be a person who would welcome some other kind of study group if it were available.[2] Having matters concerning discipleship as a broad heading on a PCC agenda can encourage people to think about this aspect of their church life even if it does not give rise to a lot of talk.

Some might like to use the term 'teaching' to describe this aspect of the church's life; teaching being a term in common use whereas 'discipleship' is confined to Christian circles and might seem a little heavy. However, sermons are not the same thing as lectures and talking about teaching can make some people feel the same dread and fear they had when they were at school. The very first Christians were described as disciples, and a disciple is someone who aims to learn from the master. Perhaps 'discipleship' is not an ideal term for this aspect of the church's life. Study, learning, education, training? Maybe there is no ideal word for this activity, but it is a part of what being a church has been about from the beginning.

Resources

If the various aspects of a church life are clustered together under these three headings for consideration by a local church council there are still going to be some which do not fit. These might be the subjects which normally take up a lot of discussion time at meetings: building repairs, the money in the accounts, cutting the grass in the churchyard, repairing the hassocks, the state of the hymnbooks, maintaining the boiler and organising the church cleaning rota. The church that St Paul wrote to in Corinth did not have to worry about these things but most churches in England are going to have to think about some of them. Some church members find it frustrating that their church's life seems to be dominated by such matters. Others do not mind it at all because these are the things they find it easier to think about. Thinking about God is not easy. Lawnmowers are much simpler. However, there are some people, and not all of them clergy, who find it much easier talking about God than dealing with a temperamental mower.

This fourth area of concern for a PCC is its resources. It is easy for a church council to slip into the mode of feeling that all this business of getting churchyards cut, maintaining the organ, servicing or replacing the boiler, repairing the building and keeping the church clean, not to speak of raising the money to pay for these things and the parish's contribution to the diocese, is all a great chore. Enthusiastic church members can feel they are a distraction from the real task of the church. And they might be a chore. They might be a distraction. But these things are also possible resources for the church to use. It sometimes needs a URC minister to say to them that he'd give his right arm to have a beautiful medieval building like theirs for them to realise this thing is not necessarily a burden but also something attractive which speaks of centuries of prayer and the worship of God. Methodist and Baptist churches would sometimes love to have the ready connections with a local community which the Church of England has through its traditions of church weddings and funerals.

Whilst a churchyard can be a drab place it can also sometimes be a bright public space which is rich with memories as well as flowers and birdlife.

The Diocese of Hereford some years ago produced a small resource book for people visiting churches to browse. They called it *A Place to Dream*.[3] People like to visit church buildings, often people who rarely go to church for services. These churches can be places where people's imaginations might be caught by artistic details in the stonework or the colour in windows and then opened out to the past, the future and to big questions.

Not all church buildings can necessarily do this. In some places they cannot be left open during the day, although most rural churches can. And some churches are not attractive. Others cost so much to repair and maintain that the PCC needs to ask basic questions about whether it really is the best use of their time and energy considering that fundamentally their task is about God's love for the world and not repairing historical stonework. The church is about building community, about prayer and worship and working out how they can best be disciples of Jesus Christ in their own place and time. The building, the boiler and the churchyard may be a burden they would be better off without, though they may also be resources for their essential tasks.

The people

Like any organisation its principal resource is its people. In the case of a church it is its members, among whom is its vicar. The vicar is not the church. The vicar is there to work with the church. According to the Church of England's Synodical Government Measure of 1969 the essential task of the Parochial Church Council is to co-operate with the vicar 'in promoting in the parish the whole mission of the church: pastoral, evangelistic, social and ecumenical'. Its functions also include 'consideration and discussion of matters concerning the Church of England or any other matter of religious or public interest'; and it is the duty of the vicar and the PCC 'to consult together on matters of general concern and importance to the parish'.[4] The mission of the church is not a clearly defined task which can be ticked off a list once it has been done. It is broad, involving community development and pastoral care, worship and prayer, teaching and learning, and people helping each other to grasp something more of the good news about God. And in this, both by the foundational idea of what the church is, by its tradition of having both clergy and lay leaders and by legislation such as this Measure, the vicar and the lay church members are clearly meant to work together.

In hard cash terms the vicar is also probably the church's most expensive resource. Most country churches pay more in their parish share to the diocese than they do in an average year even on building repairs. And most of that parish share goes towards paying the clergy. On financial grounds alone it only makes sense for a local church to help its vicar work most efficiently and effectively. That is not likely to happen when the vicar is left to just get on with everything on his or her own, or is pushed into doing things that he or she cannot do effectively or that other people can do better. It is likely to happen best when the vicar has other people to work with when necessary and above all when the vicar is able to work out amongst all the multitude of things that could be done which are the most important.

The vicar

Looking at the church's life in this way, as a collaborative venture, the vicar comes into it not necessarily as the focus of the church or in the vanguard of its mission, but as one participant in what the local church is doing. The vicar will no doubt contribute to discussion and decision-making in many areas, and may head up particular pieces of work, but the vicar is not doing it all. That is not only impossible, practically, but it goes against the idea of the church as a group or network of people.

The vicar never is doing all the church's work and both clergy and lay people need to remember that. The most energetic and conscientious country parsons are kidding themselves if they think that they are carrying out the church's ministry. At the very least they are ignoring the multitude of conversations which go on between neighbours and the prayers of the people who join them on a Sunday morning. But in any parish now the vicar might contribute by organising or leading a particular piece of work or by being the focal person for a regular activity like the Sunday worship. Or the vicar might simply join in with what someone else is organising or leading. The vicar might simply be there when it happens or might not even do that.

In one particular parish in a group the vicar might organise the harvest festival service together with several other people. When they meet to plan the vicar might be the person who is able to tell others about the state of health of one of their normally active church members who was recently rushed into hospital, although it may have been someone else who actually visited her. The vicar might later look at and enjoy the harvest decorations and attend the supper whilst leaving a churchwarden to organise the auction of produce and leaving the treasurer to send off the collection to Christian Aid afterwards.

However, in another parish the situation might be quite different. There the same vicar might be organising a social function because the church membership desperately needs a good knees-up and no one else is in a fit state to do it. In another church that vicar might teach a new hymn to a congregation once a month, which is unnecessary in yet another church which has a choir and competent organist, and would be impossible in a third one because the congregation there would refuse to open their mouths.

So the vicar works in conjunction with other church members. There is a difference in that the vicar is paid a stipend to do church work whereas the others are usually volunteers. The vicar has particular legal responsibilities, some of which are shared with the churchwardens and PCC and some of which are the vicar's alone. Also a great number of expectations are laid on the vicar by church members and other parishioners, some of which cannot possibly be met. The

93

question is: how does the vicar find a way through this? How does the vicar work out what to do and what to leave? Or how can churches and their vicar work together so that the vicar is able to make the best use of his or her skills and expertise and provide the local churches with the support and help that they need?

The strength of George Herbert's seventeenth-century idea of the Country Parson was that it was a clear image. When he was writing his suggestion was not part of the mainstream thinking of the Church of England but it became so in due course and provided the principal model for many generations of country clergy. Though some still want to present it as the key image of what an ordained minister working in a rural area should be about, this is a very different time and a different way of thinking is now needed. The best of Herbert's ideal can be retained but the fundamental idea will not be of a country parson doing the church's work but of a vicar in a group of parishes working with lay church members.

The Agenda

Widderton PCC 18 September 2002 at The Hollies

1.   *INTRODUCTION*
1.1   *Opening prayer*
1.2   *Apologies for absence*
1.3   *Minutes of PCC meeting on 3 July (circulated)*

2.   *COMMUNITY*
2.1   *Nigeria link: letter from Joseph Yisa in Minna*
2.2   *Churches Together Christmas Bazaar: report from planning group*
2.3   *Skittles evening: report and review*
2.4   *Any other Community matters*

4.   *WORSHIP*
4.1   *Songs of Praise: review*
4.2   *Plans for Harvest Service and Supper: planning group to report*
4.3   *Outline plans for Advent and Christmas*
4.4   *Deanery Confirmation: Thursday 17 October, 7.00 p.m. at Dorminster*
4.5   *Any other worship matters*

5.   *DISCIPLESHIP*
5.1   *Basic Christianity Course: Report from Paul Teecham*
5.2   *Sunday Club: Report from Jean Bladgett*
5.3   *'On the Way': Vicar to report on this diocesan initiative*

5.4 Marriage of divorcees in church: Vicar to report
5.5 Any other discipleship matters

6. RESOURCES
6.1 Financial Report: Treasurer
6.2 Progress report on work on tower and clock: Report from Jim Winder
6.3 Heating improvement possibilities: Report from Jack Cole
6.4 Replacement of stolen chairs: Churchwardens

7. OTHER BUSINESS
7.1 Any other matters arising from the minutes of 3 July
7.2 Correspondence
7.3 Any other business

8. NEXT MEETING: Wednesday 13 November at Brightside Farm

6

Twelve Apostles

In a working day a country vicar will spend some time on the phone. Some of those calls might be about events that are coming up, some might involve mainly listening to someone talking about their recent bereavement or a worry they have for one of their family. Some might be from someone in the diocesan administration, or a monumental mason, or a prospective bride about a wedding. The vicar's day is likely to also include some meetings, maybe pre-arranged – several people in a room discussing the business of a church or the local school – some might be chance conversations. Some conversations will be the result of the vicar deliberately calling on a parishioner. Some time is likely to be spent at the computer or typewriter dealing with correspondence.

During the day the vicar will also probably be thinking over possibilities for the next sermon or school assembly and will spend some time in prayer. No two days will be the same, and in these various situations each day the vicar is going to take on different roles. At times the vicar will be a manager or administrator, at others a teacher or pastor, at others a priest, an evangelist, a social activist or a church representative. There are a dozen roles a vicar might take.

Manager
As a manager the vicar's concern is that the church works effectively. In the nineteenth century vicars established and managed schools, they saw to the reordering of churches, they established an annual church fete and made sure that

each person knew what they needed to do to make it a success. They established Sunday Schools and made sure there were teachers, and outings. The manager's concern now is likely to be that people are involved in the life of the church, that morale is good and that each person knows what he or she is meant to be doing.

The manager will spend time with active church members one-to-one or in meetings, smoothing out disagreements, trying to resolve disputes, affirming and encouraging people in what they are doing and recruiting people for vacancies. Five parishes have ten churchwardens, five treasurers and five secretaries. And whilst the vicar may well leave the Annual Parochial Church Meeting to sort out its own PCC members, it is likely that the manager will want to be prepared and have already found people willing to take on these other crucial jobs.

Wanting to see the church as the Body of Christ with all its limbs and organs working in a healthy way, the manager will tap into the various resources available which might help in this. Learning from the expertise of others with a similar concern, the manager-vicar may consult some of the many handbooks written over the years giving advice on such things as church meetings, time management, filing systems and how early to arrive at a church before a service. The manager may have worked with a management consultant or have studied for an MBA. The manager might have drawn up job descriptions for churchwardens and PCC members, because, despite the fact that every year thirty thousand churchwardens are elected across England and every time a person is asked by a vicar whether they are willing to become churchwarden the person will invariably say 'What does it involve?', the church has no standard statement of the churchwarden's job. There are books written in various styles from the jolly enthusiastic to the turgid legalese, but there is no succinct statement. The manager might produce other documents which might help the other people involved in the running of the local churches.

Administrator

The administrator meanwhile is more concerned with organising things, the resources of the church and the community, because if things are in a mess there is friction, time is wasted, and frustration grows. Administrators know that among the earliest lists of roles within the church they are mentioned. St Paul lists administrators with apostles and prophets, and on official documents down the centuries in England the vicar has been styled a 'clerk in holy orders'. It is a time-honoured role within the church.

Though scorned by some the administrator knows that the church cannot present itself and Christ well if there is bad administration as people are let down by it. If their letters are not answered, their phone messages are not returned, their e-mails never read, their wedding planning seems to be haphazard, or they are not told things they need to know, people feel they do not matter and their concerns and their contribution to the church's life are of no account.

Leader

While the administrator might be happy with a low profile within the community, quietly working away to make sure that things run smoothly, the leader needs to be visible. The leader is concerned to take the church forward, or to navigate its way through storms, encouraging, but also giving direction. As the old King James Version put it, 'Where there is no vision the people perish' (Proverbs 29:18). The leader has the vision, shares the vision and inspires people to work towards it. The leader spends less time looking at the management manuals and more reading the Bible, church history, biographies and inspirational books. The story of the church is one of movement, change and heroes: George Whitefield and George MacLeod, John Henry Newman and Trevor Huddleston.

The leader attends meetings, either to be up front or to contribute ideas and try to steer from the side. The leader writes lively articles in magazines and preaches with vigour. For the leader the church is an army on the move, or a band of pilgrims on its way to a promised land.

Church representative

The vicar might take very seriously the minister's role as a representative of the church. The church needs to be visible within the wider community and the vicar is the one to make sure that happens. So the vicar as the church's representative writes to the local papers and sends out press releases, always ready to answer questions from reporters. The representative will do a television interview if there is some noteworthy local issue or event and contribute to local radio discussion. The representative will be at meetings of the local council and maybe organise a forum of candidates when there is an election.

The church represents God in the world and in this mode the vicar represents the church. Spokesperson or advocate, this is a time-honoured role in England. Bishops still sit in the House of Lords, chair commissions and investigations, facilitate meetings with government ministers or get reported for their views on ethical matters. The vicar does a similar job at the local level. As a representative of the church the vicar takes very seriously the way the church is seen, or is sometimes regrettably invisible, and the fact that people who are not active members will still take note of what the church thinks and does.

Pastor

The pastor has a different focus. The pastor is concerned with the spiritual growth of the church, of the individuals that are its members and of those who have little to do with it but who all matter infinitely to God. The pastor wants to see growth in faith and in holiness, or in wholeness. The two words are not related etymologically though the two concepts are connected. Holiness implies a close connection with God and the better one is in touch with God the more whole one becomes. The pastor is concerned with healing of the spirit, mind, soul and body, although the pastor will be aware of the expertise of others in different fields and not want to move beyond his or her own level of competence. The vicar as pastor will complement the work of physicians and psychotherapists.

Down the centuries there has been a continual stream of church ministers who have seen themselves first and foremost as pastors. Twenty years younger than George Herbert was Richard Baxter, a puritan who believed in monarchy and a humble episcopacy, who served for seventeen years as the vicar of Kidderminster in Worcestershire and inspired other clergy in the area with his devotion as a pastor to his parishioners. Among his many writings was *The Reformed Pastor*, a guide to the organisation and practice of helping people grow in holiness.

The pastor may have some training in counselling beyond the rather rudimentary work done at a theological college. Pastors are likely to take very seriously their own prayer life and their study of spiritual writings, and to attend retreats and quiet days. For them the church grows as people respond to the promptings of the Holy Spirit and their aim is to assist in this prompting and this response.

Evangelist

Some vicars see themselves principally as evangelists. The focus of the evangelist will be people but with less emphasis on their growth in the Spirit and more on their conversion to Christ in the first place. The evangelist's driving concern is not principally that people need to grow in holiness but that they need to hear the gospel of God's love and turn to Christ in faith. Clearly there is not a contradiction here between the pastor and the evangelist, but a different focus. Both pastors and evangelists feature in St Paul's writings in the New Testament. Traditionally the evangelist has been more concerned to share the good news with those who have not heard it. The pastor is more concerned to build up the faith of those who have heard and responded. And while down the centuries pastors have often been rooted in a particular community, evangelists have often moved around as wandering friars or itinerant missionaries.

101

In some churches in the Anglican Communion these are clearly separate ministries. The Anglican Church in rural Nigeria has people who are authorised evangelists, who go out to other villages within their area, talking and preaching. There are others who are authorised pastors, whose task is to care for and build up the congregation in their village. Neither are ordained. The ordained minister is the local vicar who has overall responsibility for perhaps twenty or thirty churches.

In England the vicar-evangelist is likely to focus on building links with people who are not already involved in the church's life, and is willing to engage in conversations about God, life, death, and maybe sin, at any time that the others want to talk about these things. The evangelist has a strong sense that people suffer if they do not know the love of God in their lives. The evangelist wants them to hear the good news, whether it be in conversation, magazine articles, baptism visits, or in addresses at funerals or on any other occasions they happen to be at the church.

Teacher and trainer

Some vicars will see the lay church members as the people best able to act as evangelists. It is they who are living and working with people who are not church members. And many people see it as the vicar's job to believe in God and try to get people to come to church. Lay church members can speak without the taint of vested interest.

But if lay church members are to do this they need to be confident about what they believe, and it is up to the vicar to help them in this. Some vicars will not want church members to be able to just talk about God but to relate their faith to the issues they face in their work and home lives. Others will want them to be able to take an active part in the life of their local church with confidence, knowing what they are doing, able to take initiatives, and moving towards a position where they can be the local leaders and ministers of the church.

All this calls for teaching and training, and some vicars, or all vicars on some occasions, will see themselves as teachers.

For many country vicars over the centuries this was confined to preparing the young for confirmation and preaching each Sunday. Though evangelicals might have wanted to hold midweek Bible studies and some Anglo-Catholics meditation on the sacrament and teaching about prayer, it is hard to judge how successful they would have been in nineteenth-century English villages.

But in the twentieth century came an increase in Lent groups, people willing to meet for study during the six weeks before Easter if at no other time. From suburban churches came the idea of housegroups, which flourished in some rural places as well. And many people followed courses like Alpha, Emmaus and other local varieties, took part in forums on social issues or matters of local concern, and in most dioceses the basic theology course which provided the material for training as a Reader was also followed by many other people as well.

The Class was the mainstay of the Methodist movement. It provided the local framework for pastoral care and the expectation and the context for adult Bible study and learning. From the Class came the local church leadership, independent of its minister in a way beyond the reckoning or the comfort zone of most Church of England clergy. The structure of the Church of England is different but the Church of England in rural areas has moved into a situation whereby the local vicar, like the Methodist minister a century ago, has to support a cluster of different churches in different communities. And many rural vicars see it as a priority that these churches have a degree of independence and self-confidence, otherwise they will cease to exist. Members of these churches will only gain the skills and confidence they need with some form of teaching and training. For some country vicars these are a priority.

Chaplain

There is also a long tradition in the Church of England of the vicar being available for people when needed. The chaplain in the hospital, the army, the prison or the college was not someone weighed down with administrative, management or teaching responsibilities, but someone with time to meet with people when they needed it and to meet them where they were, be it the hospital bed, the mess, the cell, or by the porter's office. The country vicar might take on this chaplain role within a cluster of villages.

The vicar might be the chaplain to the farmers, the hunt, the village school, the quarry, the small factory, the senior citizen's club, the housebound elderly or the day centre. Maybe the vicar would try to be the chaplain to everyone, making a point of visiting houses, calling in the pubs and the schools and the places people work, being at village events or at the Post Office or the shop when other people are likely to be there.

As chaplain the vicar might get to know of the needs of people within a community and be able to speak for them. To the parish council the vicar might speak of the need for affordable housing, to the PCC of the needs of families with young children. Where a church is predominantly people with a professional or business background the chaplain may be aware of the very different values of the local working class.

In chaplain mode the vicar might occasionally need to act as a mediator, perhaps between parents and a school head or between groups with strongly opposed views over a local development or proposed event. The chaplain is not on anyone's side, and in the same way that the hospital chaplain is not running the hospital the vicar as chaplain will not be running the church. In the Royal Navy chaplains have no rank but take the rank of the person they are talking to. So the vicar as chaplain will belong to no social grouping in the parish but will hope to relate equally to any of them. The focus of the chaplain's attention will be the people in the community and so they would go with the view that the church's task is seeing what God is doing and joining in. Like the industrial chaplain who not only aims to meet with people in their place of work but also to bring Christian theology to bear on the issues of the workplace, the country vicar as chaplain is trying to see local issues and concerns in the light of Christian teaching, and to help others do so as well.

Priest

For the priest, however, there is likely to be more of a concern with the church. All Church of England vicars are, technically, priests. Usually twelve months after being ordained deacon, while they are still a curate, they are ordained priest. According to the Oxford English Dictionary the English word 'priest' derives ultimately from the ecclesiastical Latin *presbyter*, which comes from the Greek word *presbyteros*, which is usually translated 'elder'. Whereas the *Book of Common Prayer* was happy referring to priests, the Alternative Service Book of 1980 subtitled the ordination service with the explanation that priests were 'also called presbyters'. Behind this lies a historical division within the Church of England.

In Greek there was another word, *hiereus*, which referred to a religious functionary who said prayers and made sacrifices and generally acted as a mediator between the people and their god. It was the word used of the Hebrew priests when the Hebrew Scriptures were translated into Greek some two centuries before Christ. Some clergy would see themselves as Christ's representatives within the parish, and as Christ fulfilled this intermediary task of the Hebrew priests of the Old Testament, so they too are fulfilling that task. They would see themselves as intermediaries between people and God, particularly as they pray for the people of the parish and preside at the sacraments. Others, however, say, No, there is no intermediary necessary. Christ himself is the one High Priest and each person can have direct access to God through Christ. No other intermediary is necessary. They say that for ministers to think they need to stand between people and God belittles the work of Christ.

In the past this disagreement has been bloody. It was one of the major issues at the Reformation. Now life in the Church of England is much more congenial and the disagreement settles down to a difference of opinion or emphasis. Most in the former camp, who are at the Catholic wing of the church, would say, 'Of course any person can have direct access to God in their prayers but God, through the Church, still appoints some to have this representative and intermediary function, with the authority to forgive sins and to preside at the eucharist.' Meanwhile most at the other end, in the evangelical wing, would say that all believers are priests, in that all Christians can represent Christ to another person at any time, but that those who have positions of leadership in the church are often seen by people as also representing God, and so their words and actions have this function. And the rules of the church state quite clearly that only those ordained priest, or presbyter, can preside at the Holy Communion anyway.

What it comes to is that some clergy will place more emphasis than others on this aspect of their ministry in which they are a representative of God and have the God-given authority to declare forgiveness, pronounce blessing and preside at the Holy Communion. They are likely to have a strong sense that God is made known to the world through the worship of the church, and as the person authorised to oversee and preside in worship they are going to take this task very seriously. The church has been given the sacraments as means of God's grace. In a sense therefore the church is itself sacramental. Its whole life, and especially its worship, is to be a means of grace. The priest therefore also has a sacramental role, representing God to the world.

In the middle of the twentieth century some Roman Catholic priests in France took on secular employment and became known as 'worker priests'. Unlike evangelists who might well take on any job in order to be able to talk with the people in that situation and share something of the gospel with them, the worker priests were principally there to represent God, to be present in the workplace, and so to help the people be closer to God. Clearly talking might come into it, but the emphasis was the sacramental presence of the priest in the secular work situation. Similarly the country vicar with that emphasis might go into the local pubs, attend village events and visit, not principally as a way of being available to people, like the chaplain, or to build up links which can then be developed in conversations about God, like the evangelist, but simply to be there and let it be known by their presence that God is interested and concerned about this aspect of life as well as what happens in the church. In fact God is present in this aspect of life, and not just in the church.

Many parishioners who do not have a clear sacramental theology will also see it this way. The vicar represents God and it is good that he takes an interest. Most parishes will have tales told with enthusiasm of a vicar who used to drink regularly in the local pub and was a good chap. Nobody can remember him ever talking about God, but that didn't matter. In fact it was probably better that he didn't. The important thing was that he was there, unlike another vicar who kept himself apart, possibly preparing sermons and services, leading Bible studies, dealing with copious correspondence and raising money for overseas missions but all unknown to the villagers beyond the church circle. This other one was also much more inclined to talk embarrassingly about God when he met you.

Liturgist

It is not only those vicars who have a strong sense of themselves as priests who see the church's worship as being important. All vicars will spend some time each week preparing for the services on Sunday. The services out of the old Book of Common Prayer are the easiest. The form is given, there are very few options and the readings are set in the lectionary, together with a psalm. All that is needed is to prepare a sermon and decide the hymns and the prayers.

Vicars can choose whatever hymns they wish. While the church has agonised long and hard over the finer points of its published prayers there has never been an authorised or even a recommended hymnbook. Hymns come and hymns go. Some go on for a long time. Some are sung once only and then forgotten.

Hymn singing took off in England in the 1700s but not initially in the Church of England. There were those who believed that only the Bible should be sung and so the earliest hymns in the Church of England, as in the Presbyterian churches, were psalms and other passages from the Bible. But gradually new hymns came on stream, filtering into the Church of England from the Methodists and other Nonconformists. By the end of the nineteenth century hymn singing was assumed.

There was a time in the mid twentieth century when churches generally sang from either *Hymns Ancient and Modern* or *The English Hymnal*, with a few avante garde congregations using *Songs of Praise*. Between these there was a lot of common ground. Hymns by people like Percy Dearmer and Jan Struther slowly crept into the congregational repertoire, often through school worship. New arrangements were made of old words and some new hymns were written but then from the 1970s onwards there was a flood of songs for worship.

There is now greater diversity and less common ground. What one congregation might think of as 'what everyone knows' might actually be totally unknown to another group of regular worshippers. 'Majesty' and 'The Servant King' would be old hymns, passé even, to some congregations, but unknown innovations to others who love 'Now thank we all our God' and 'Angel voices ever singing', which the others have never heard of.

Any vicar starting in a new parish will very quickly find out what forms of service the congregations are familiar with, and what they prefer and dislike. More time will have to be spent discovering the hymn repertoire of the congregations. The vicar might be able to choose any hymn but it doesn't mean the congregation is going to sing it. And even when the vicar is very familiar with a parish there will be surprising moments when a hymn the vicar had assumed all the world knew appears to be a total mystery to the congregation.

With *Common Worship*, preparing a service became more complicated. A service needs to be worked out from among a million options although most village churches by now probably have a form of service they are reasonably comfortable with, which does not need redesigning every week.[1] In fact, they probably don't want it to change much but find the familiarity helpful.

It is the other services which take much more time and these are often the ones to which people come who are not particularly familiar with the regular Sunday fare. From the nineteenth-century development of Harvest Thanksgiving and carol services there has been a steady growth of less formal services in the rural Church of England. Medieval agricultural festivals like Lammastide and Plough Sunday have been resurrected. Rogation Sunday, once a time for a service in church and then the beating of the bounds to familiarise parishioners with the limits of their territory, has in places turned into a procession around the farms or other places of work in a parish, or an outdoor service in one significant location. The country vicar is given ample scope for developing skills as a liturgist in responding to the need for all-age worship, baptism services which are accessible to occasional church attenders, Christingles, school services and Remembrance Sunday, together with possible celebrations of Candlemas, May Day, All Saints, All Souls and the local patron saint, as well as pet services, craft fairs, music and arts festivals and requests for special services by local organisations.

These all demand time and attention. Such events cannot be worked out with a simple cut-and-paste job on *Common Worship* on a Saturday morning. They require planning, thought, a sense of shape and movement and music, a familiarity with a range of resources from different publishers and maybe websites, a knowledge of what might work with a particular group, and often the involvement of other people.

Some vicars will want to take this further, developing liturgies which take hold of the deep experiences of people and offer them to God. For some funerals and weddings people want something familiar. They want Psalm 23 sung to Crimond and 'Abide with me' at the funeral, and 'Praise, my soul' at the wedding, having walked in to Wagner's Bridal March from *Lohengrin*. But some people do not want this. They want a service that is personal and relates to their circumstances. And although the forms are prescribed, and in the case of a wedding cannot legally be altered too much, there is still some scope for developing a service which fits a particular situation.

There are occasions for which there is not a set liturgy. Increasing numbers of clergy now tap into the resources of the Iona Community for prayers, readings, or simple liturgies for particular occasions, prayers for healing, prayers of pilgrimage and journeying, liturgies for justice and peace or for respect for creation. Many of these prayers and services are not devised by the Community on the Hebridean island of Iona but by people working in local churches, often in Scottish cities but also in many other parts of the world. They come from community members holding workshops in churches, developing ideas with other people, trying them out, reshaping them, and finally sometimes publishing the result after a period of trial and testing. The prayers, blessings and liturgies come from the experiences and concerns of people both within and outside local churches.

Some country vicars will want to do this kind of work: writing new hymns and prayers for special occasions or perhaps composing a liturgy or prayers about a local issue or crisis, or together with a family that is in the midst of a crisis or which wants to express its sense of relief and gratitude following a period of stress or anxiety. This is a development of the church's pastoral work. In the past a lot of pastoral work has related to the ongoing worship of the church in its established and given forms and often that continues to be adequate for the task. But sometimes vicars want to take this further. Perhaps they feel that something is happening which can be taken up creatively into a new form of worship. In such a situation the vicar will be a facilitator, maybe the one who knows what is already available, and who with the skills of a liturgist can help people find a way of offering their experience to God in worship.

Social activist

Some vicars will not be comfortable with a focus solely on worship and the life of the church. The message of Jesus was

110

about the kingdom of God. The prophets before him were concerned with justice. Jesus taught a way of peace, and had a passion for the reconciliation of factions, healed the sick and fed the hungry. In Luke's gospel he began his work by reading from the prophet Isaiah about the blind seeing, the deaf hearing, the lame able to walk, and the arrival of the day of the Lord, the day of Jubilee and liberation. And for some vicars that should be the focus of the church's life.

They may see their role as being to encourage and support church members in their own involvement within the local community, in local politics and pressure groups, in business or trade union activity, in charities, fair trade campaigning and support networks. They might see a need to get involved themselves, leading from the front in lobbying, organising and campaigning.

The vicar as social activist has a long history. One of the leaders of the fourteenth-century peasants' revolt was a clergyman. The tensions between Puritan and Laudian during the seventeenth century were not just about preferences in liturgy but about different visions of how society should be. In the nineteenth century while some clergy were vigorously defending the established social order, others worked to produce gradual change through education and welfare, and some wanted radical change, though these were more likely to be found in the Nonconformist churches. But the social activist vicar of today can also look back to Anglicans like John Newton, Charles Kingsley and F. D. Maurice struggling to improve society for the poorest when many others saw poverty at the rich man's gate as part of God's established order.

Lifestyler

Also to be found amongst the country clergy is the lifestyler, who sees his or her response to God as being not principally a matter of doing things but of being something. The Christian, as this person sees it, is not called to frenetic activity but to be fully human. And in a society in which people are dehumanised by the incessant demands of work or their response to the lure of ever increasing wealth the church must be an alternative community. The characteristics of the church are to be a balanced and wholesome life.

Lifestylers can look back to the Benedictines of the Middle Ages with their regular pattern of work and prayer. They might look at the rural world of the eighteenth and nineteenth century and see that as a place where the pace of life was slower and more human and people were not alienated from the land or their labour. They might look to the alternative lifestyle movement as it developed in America and Europe from the 1960s onwards, combining a way of living with a concern for the needs of the poor and exploited.

The alternative lifestyler might use the vicarage garden to develop a degree of self-sufficiency in vegetables and fruit, keeping chickens and maybe a goat and buying only fair-traded and organic foods, maybe keeping to a vegetarian diet and eschewing caffeine and other stimulants. The cultured lifestyler might go for a life of gentle socialising, painting, writing, travelling to the city for the theatre or a concert and perhaps wanting to encourage others in a similar way through music-making or a book group. The family lifestyler vicar will be there at the school gate or the bus stop, not simply to chat with the other parents but to collect their own children who will then have their time and attention for the evening. No church events will happen between four and seven, at least not involving them, and evening events will be limited as their partner and children need their time as much, or more, than the local churches.

Which role?

No vicar is going to get by taking on just one of these roles. Some roles will be thrust on unsuspecting ministers against their wishes. The vicar who wants to sees herself as the pastor of the flocks will have to spend some time dealing with paper, filing, forms, registers, correspondence and phone calls attending to matters of gravestones, wedding music, attendance figures and faculties. The chaplain who wishes to stay quietly available, a specialist in corner conversations about significant matters, will sometimes have to step forward and represent the church to the local radio or press. The evangelist who sees himself as one of the church, a friend and companion with a particular gift for helping people come to know Christ in a personal way, will find that at times he has to be formal and up front, representing God and the church as the parish priest.

There might be other roles, chosen by or thrust upon the country vicar. The vicar might be everyone's uncle, an agony aunt, a social worker, a saviour, or the new romantic interest in a tight-knit community. The vicar might be seen and treated as a fool or a freeloader. Some of these the vicar might resent. Some they might be happy with. Some roles they might take reluctantly but realise the roles are necessary for the time or that plenty of people before them were cast in the same role, including perhaps Jesus and the apostles.

What is most likely to happen is that one or two of the possible roles become predominant. These take most of the time or most of the energy while others slip into the background, only occasionally taking centre stage when the situation demands it or the vicar is particularly smitten by a neglected need. Vicars will all have a few roles which they see as the most important ones for them to take, or the ones in which they feel most comfortable.

The question is: how is it to be worked out which of these various possible roles should be the principal ones for a particular vicar in a particular place? Is it for the vicar to decide, and if so, how? Or should the local congregation or its representatives have some say in this and take some responsibility for helping the vicar juggle conflicting demands and decide priorities? Or is this something that should be laid down in a job description or an instruction from the bishop?

If the vicar is not to be seen as the church personified but as a member of the church taking different roles and contributing to the life of the church in various ways, then the vicar needs to be able to sort out with other people how he or she is to work. But the church as a whole and the clergy in particular are not used to that. Many clergy will be anxious at the thought, fearing they will lose their independence or become even more burdened by unrealistic expectations. Ways of doing this need to be found which will not restrict the creativity of the clergy or burden them with impossible ideals but help them make the best use of their gifts in collaboration with both the local and the wider church.

Trainers

Archdeacon Richard Cutter was silent for the first five minutes of his lasagne. Jane, his wife, talked about meeting Cecilia Wingfield at the Oxfam shop and the new line of Fairtrade teas that the Co-op were now selling. Then, Richard said, 'I saw a curate this morning.'

'Are they rare?' said Jane.

'This one was. He wore trainers. Apparently he always wears trainers. Even at funerals.'

'Just trainers?'

'Now that's an interesting thought. No, cassock and surplice and trainers.'

'And?'

'And the clients don't like it very much. I had a letter complaining.'

'What about his vicar?'

'I spoke to him. And he's already talked with his curate about this several times and can't get anywhere. So I said I'd see him.'

He took another mouthful of lunch, and chewed, thinking of curates. 'He said it was a matter of integrity. He was someone who wore trainers. That's what he was. He was young. Young people wear trainers. If he was a monk and wore sandals would I object? Probably not, I said, because that is a well-established custom. But he is the new generation. Trainers. And an earring.'

'No one complains about the earring?'

'Apparently not. But they feel he's disrespectful to the deceased wearing trainers at a funeral.'

'Could he see that?'

'No, he reckoned it'd be more disrespectful if he pretended to be something he wasn't.'

'Like someone who wears shoes?'

'Quite.'

'Isn't there some rule or other? About trainers?'

'The canons talk about appropriate and distinctive dress. They don't specify "No trainers". Neither do the diocesan guidelines on professional behaviour. They don't say you mustn't take baptisms wearing overalls and a safety helmet either. One assumes a certain degree of sensitivity and common sense.

'So I told him about when I was a young vicar and had to take the funeral of an old man who'd been a singer. He'd been well known around the clubs in the Midlands in his day. And his son wanted us to play the Frank Sinatra song, "I did it my way". So I started to explain how we couldn't do that because it wasn't a Christian attitude. And the son said, "Whose bloody funeral is it?" And that stopped me in my tracks.'

'So what did you do?'

'I let them play Frank Sinatra.'

'And did the curate get the point?'

'No. He said, "There you are then. I just want to exercise my ministry my way. Not your way."'

Richard finished his plate of lunch.

'So what did you do?'

'I told him I thought he ought to wear shiny shoes if that's what the parishioners found respectful. Or at least get some black trainers instead of his red ones.'

7

The Church and the Vicar

For many rural clergy there will be another possible role in their minds as they think about their work. That is the role of the parson. For the parson all of these other roles must be taken on, and done so graciously and effectively. They are all part of the vocation of the country vicar and all must be fulfilled for the glory of God. Rural clergy know they are not working in a rural idyll and know that their situation is very different from that of the early twentieth century, let alone the times of Chaucer or George Herbert, and yet this image of the country vicar still profoundly influences their attitude to their work. It is as if among the possible roles that they can adopt in their work they have a Parson lurking in their minds' shadows wanting and able to take over at any opportunity.

This haunting Parson can be given voice by parishioners. They will tell the active manager and administrator, who designs imaginative liturgies and is conspicuous in the local press and regularly communicates with local councillors and the MP, that a previous vicar was such a nice man who always had time for everyone. Or they will remind the pastor vicar, out in the parish at all hours, present in any crisis, always the first one to call on newcomers, rejoicing with those with a newborn child and weeping with those whose pet dog and sole companion has finally died, that you always knew what Vicar X expected you to do, or that Vicar Y produced such a wonderful carol service, involving all the children.

However, the Parson may not need parishioners to speak for him. His voice might sound in the vicar's own thoughts as

117

paperwork is neglected for a home visit, or visiting is neglected to plan a service, or a Candlemas service was not as good as it would have been if they had spent more time on that and less on preparing the Lent course, or the Lent course was not as well done as it would have been if the vicar had worked with a planning group rather than done it alone. The Parson might remind them as they drive through a village of who they have not visited, and when they are getting robed for a service of how the vestry really needs a good clear out, or when they are researching in their reference books for Sunday's sermon that there are letters which have been lying unanswered on the desk for a fortnight. But the role of the parson cannot be fulfilled.

One small village

Consider, for instance, the parish of Hamley on the edge of the Cotwolds, a pretty village of two hundred people with a few outlying cottages and farms. Several members of the parish church in Hamley met one evening to discuss how things were in their parish. There was an ongoing controversy about mud on the road and another about the smell from one of the farms but at this meeting the mud and the smell were not talked about. The situation of the farmers was discussed. The people in Hamley knew something about the problems affecting agriculture and knew the farmers concerned. They knew beef sales were picking up after BSE but the price of milk had dropped. In that area twenty years earlier many of the local councillors, churchwardens and school governors had been farmers but as times had got harder and farming more demanding the farmers had retrenched and many had become isolated.

No one knew what the malaise in agriculture meant in practice for the local farmers. There were no obvious signs of hardship but that did not mean that the accounts were healthy. They knew that the local landowner took a very personal interest in his tenants and was known to be very supportive of people in difficulties. They felt there was little that they as individuals or as a small community could do about an economic problem affecting a whole industry. They could only be aware that whilst their farming neighbours might appear to be carrying on as if business was the same as usual they might actually have serious problems.

There were others with problems too. There was the retired churchwarden who seemed to have adjusted well to not being in the thick of things but following a stroke now found fast conversation difficult. People felt for him and his wife who looked after him. She managed to have something of a social life of her own but it was obviously hard.

Then there was a former bank manager who had moved into the village some forty years before and was now blind. His wife was crippled with arthritis. Another elderly woman who had been very involved in the life of the village was now getting very confused, losing track of the day and the time, forgetting where she had put things and what bills needed to be paid. A neighbour looked in regularly to keep an eye on her.

Another elderly villager had been through a bad viral infection through the winter but was now back in action again and moderately cheerful, in a 'mustn't grumble' kind of way. But she worried about her son and grandson. The son also lived in the village, divorced and on his own, self-employed as a carpenter and joiner. His son was in prison, doing time for causing a fatal accident whilst under the influence of heroin. He was now off the heroin but he was due out soon and the fear was that the dealers would be in touch again once he was free. He would probably return to the village but there was not a lot for him to do in Hamley and there was some discussion as to how people might be able to find him gardening work.

One of the farmer's sons had recently escaped a prison sentence having trashed a pub in Stroud with a few mates, and had been charged and heavily fined. It was a worry to his father and had been in the local paper. There was also a court case coming up regarding an older couple who wanted to have the custody of two of their grandchildren whose mother clearly could not look after them. The daughter had not been seen in the village for some time and the grandparents did not know where she was now. Bill Watson's emphysema was not too bad at the moment and he was able to get out a bit. One young couple had had a baby and wanted to stay in the village but their cottage was very small and they could not afford to buy anything that might come on the market or the rent on any of the estate houses. They were hoping to be able to move into Jenny's house. Jenny had moved into the village with her two teenage children when her marriage broke up and liked it there but she did not want to move the children's schools and it was a long drive each day to take them to school and collect them, so she was moving back to the town they had come from.

It was now three years since Jane's husband had suddenly collapsed and died in the garden at the age of forty-two. She was doing OK but now her mother had had a stroke and she was doing a fifty-mile round trip each day to visit her, as well as her job as an accounts clerk. Peter was still waiting for his operation which had been put off and he was anxious about it. The Browns were moving out of Beech Farm having decided to sell up after thirty-five years. They could see no future in the farm and their son did not want to take it over. The farm sale was set for a fortnight's time. And there was a new lady who had moved into Upper Cottage a few weeks after her husband had died. People were concerned that she should be helped to meet people.

A job for a vicar?

In Hamley the vicar might become involved in any of these situations as a pastor or a chaplain, helping people through the difficulties or working to reconcile those who were at odds with each other. She would be welcome at many of the homes where there was some difficulty and at others as well. At village events, the social evenings and the monthly bar in the village hall, she would be able to engage in discussion about local issues, contributing as a community theologian. She might also have issues in which she wanted to initiate some change, such as the provision of housing for local families, the safety of the main road, or access to the farmland by walkers. The vicar might engage with social services over the support of the grandparent carers. She could represent the church when calling on people, and in leading worship and daily prayers would be very much in the role of a priest for the parish. Services would need to be prepared for each week and on occasions in Hamley people wanted to have something more imaginative or experimental and this would call for considerable preparation by the vicar. The harvest festival and carol services were particularly significant but four times a year the church had an evening service in a different style, related to a particular concern. Each week there would also be a sermon to prepare and the vicar could work with the people who ran the children's club, preparing material, teaching the children and helping the leaders develop their skills and expertise as well. The vicar could help the PCC think how the church's life might develop in the future and play a key role in helping the church communicate the gospel to those in the parish who seemed unaware of the presence and love of God.

Together with meeting regularly with the churchwardens, treasurer and secretary of the church, dealing with the mail that came to her as the local vicar, liaising with the architect and builders over the maintenance of the building and developing the idea of installing a toilet and improving the access, helping in church fundraising and setting aside time for study, this could be a full-time job for a conscientious parson. The vicar could say morning prayers as people were leaving for work and evening prayer as they came home. If evening visits or meetings were needed she could take time off in lieu in the afternoon to do shopping or work in the garden and have one day free each week. She might have time to join a local choir or drama group, keep in touch with friends and give her family time when they were around. And she would be doing what many people would expect of her as a country parson.

However, Hamley is not an isolated parish with its own vicar. It is the smallest parish in a group of four with a total population ten times that of Hamley. I have changed the names and details to save embarrassment to the residents but it is a snapshot of a real place at a particular moment in time and these difficulties, crises and community issues are not exceptional for a rural community. Similar things would be found among any sample of two hundred people in that group of parishes, together with some considerably worse. Hamley at that moment in time had no bankruptcies or redundancies, no breaking marriages that other people knew about, no one coping with terminal cancer, no recent suicide and no one suffering acute depression. There was no known domestic violence, no burglaries, robberies or housefires. And at that time no one was preparing for a baptism or confirmation, planning a wedding and no one had recently died. It was all fairly quiet.

Across the group of parishes there would be several major crises at any one time and always some people preparing for a baptism, a wedding or a funeral. A group of parishes that size could expect to average one baptism, one wedding and two funerals a month. The pastoral needs of the people in the whole group of parishes would be at least ten times those of Hamley on that particular evening. The total amount of church work relating to services, preaching, developing liturgy, caring for buildings and dealing with administration and management matters would be four times that of Hamley.

If Hamley might make a possible full-time job for a conscientious country parson, two such parishes certainly would and it must be impossible for a vicar to work in a bigger group of parishes in the same way. Some time would certainly be saved by work being done for one church being transferable or adaptable for others: hymn selection, sermon preparation, some special services, liaison with the diocese and involvement in the deanery chapter and synod. But other things would multiply, particularly the work of finding people to take services when the vicar could not be there. This would only be holidays and illness in the single parish or in a small group of two or three. But with four or more it would be each week unless the number of services was reduced to fit with what the vicar could manage, which was probably no more than three on a Sunday. Being the vicar of four small parishes is a different job from being the vicar of one or two even if the four are very small. Four parishes and two thousand people is normal for a rural group. Many are bigger and many more will be in the future.

But many clergy still try to be the parson for their group of parishes. They try to take on all the possible roles of the vicar in all their parishes and work very long hours. One theme of the recent television programmes on country clergy was the way they seemed to work all hours and the anxiety that this caused their partners. At the same time parson vicars do not do all the work they could. They might spend a lot of time in pastoral work with their parishioners but that is still only a small fraction of what could be done. There is always more that could be done in developing the liturgy, in community involvement, in simply meeting to talk with people about local issues as a community theologian, or in teaching courses and leading study groups. And any life they have beyond their work is squeezed into odd corners.

This cannot be a good thing and it cannot be sustainable. People can work extremely long hours for short periods of time but they cannot keep it up indefinitely. Finally they burn out, become depressed, listless or lacking in creativity, imagination and humour. Or they become cynical, going through the motions and doing what is necessary but with resentment and dampening any enthusiasm that might come from someone else. Or they might bale out and do a different job instead. Jamie Allen of *A Country Parish* did not stay long in the post beyond the making of the TV series.

There are also internal tensions for a vicar as one role can pull in a different direction from another. The social activist might need to be at odds with local vested interest over a particular issue but then have to try to be a pastor to the very same people. The vicar as pastor trying to respond to the needs of all parishioners will inevitably have to work efficiently and sometimes quickly, but also needs to be able to give people time. Pastoral care is not a matter of dispensing advice or medicines to people but helping them work through from the presenting problems to the deeper issues. This can be focused but it cannot be rushed. The vicar is trying to do an enormous volume of work but in some roles the vicar needs to be available with slack time.

Such an approach cannot be good for the church either. Not only is their minister working in an ineffective way if they are trying to do the impossible but this way of doing things runs counter to the nature of the church. The vicar might represent the church but the vicar cannot be the church. The church is the community of Christians. The Apostle Paul took on a multitude of different roles at different times but still held to a view that it was the church that was the body of Christ and within the church there were a variety of different vocations. Writing to the Corinthians he says, 'You are the body of Christ and individually members of it. And God has appointed in the church first apostles, second prophets, third teachers; then deeds of power, then gifts of healing, forms of assistance, forms of leadership, various kinds of tongues. Are all apostles? Are all prophets? Are all teachers? Do all work miracles? Do all possess gifts of healing? Do all speak in tongues? Do all interpret?' (1 Corinthians 12:27–30). Clearly the implied answer is 'No, not all do.' Energetic, passionate for the gospel, willing to turn his hand and mind to whatever was necessary to build up the church, willing to be, in his words, 'all things to all people' (1 Corinthians 9:22), Paul still did not see himself as required to be the church or to do all the church's work. The church was to be all its members working together with their different gifts and opportunities.

Why the parson survives

It is worth exploring further why the image of the country parson remains so powerful even when it is impossible to fulfil and ignores the fundamental character of the church that it is not one person but the community of Christians in a place. We have noted its long history going back to the Middle Ages and the fact that it is also a simple idea which fits in well with the myth of rural England.

There are also good things about it which people want to

maintain. As described by George Herbert the parson was rooted in a particular place as a local theologian concerned with the mundane matters of rural life as well as spiritual truths; the parson was concerned with both individuals and with spiritual health of communities; the parson's life and ministry were grounded in prayer, study and worship; and the parson had a holistic approach to ministry, concerned about the physical as well as the spiritual needs of his parishioners. Many are keen to have an approach to ministry which has these characteristics and some possibly think the parson approach is the only way of doing so.

Some clergy may not realise that these were not characteristics of all country parsons of the past and were not actually maintained, even if they were achieved, by Herbert himself for more than three years. The teaching of church history in theological courses is often confined to the major intellectual movements and organisational changes in the church. The social history of the rural Church of England is not attended to and a student might not realise that the country clergy of the past were not faithfully living up to George Herbert's standard, or anything like it.

Courses at theological colleges are also often taught by people who have very little experience of parish ministry themselves, whether in a city, town or the countryside. They might have a voluntary or part-time link with a rural parish or two near the college but that does not involve them in the management of ministry in a full-sized cluster of parishes. So some clergy might choose to work in rural areas with romantic notions about country life and rural ministry which were not dispelled at theological college.

The words of the ordination service also reinforce this image of the country parson. In the service the bishop tells the priest that he or she is to work with the bishop and with fellow priests, as servant and shepherd among the people, to proclaim the word of the Lord, to call his hearers to repentance, to baptise, and to prepare the baptised for confirmation, to preside at Holy Communion, to lead people in prayer and worship, to intercede for them, to bless them, to teach

125

and encourage by word and example, to minister to the sick and prepare the dying for their death. Priests are to be messengers, watchmen and stewards of the Lord, to teach and admonish, to feed and to provide for the Lord's family, to search for God's children in the wilderness of this world's temptations and to guide them through its confusions.[1] Interestingly that is the charge regardless of whether the priest is to work in a country parish, a suburban or city church or teach in a school or college.

Situations where there was one priest for a small country parish are still within living memory, and memory is selective. Older parishioners can still remember times when the vicar on his rounds would regularly call round for a cup of tea and a chat, although that 'regularly' might have been a couple of occasions. Like the fact that summers were always sunny in the past, the churches were always full. People forget the wet summers and they remember Christmas and harvest festivals of the past, not the week-by-week services which were sometimes less well attended than they are now. But this is how some parishioners remember things and clergy, being human, often do not want to disappoint their parishioners. So they will sometimes try to do as these heroes did of old, even though they work in very different circumstances.

Parish clergy work with no appraisal scheme. They probably now have a regular ministry review but it is at best only likely to happen on an annual basis. This is an opportunity for the minister to review his or her own work. There is rarely any kind of meaningful appraisal by an archdeacon or bishop of how they are doing but, again, like anyone else, the parish clergy need affirmation. This means that some will tend to do what parishioners will thank them for, regardless of how important it actually is in the total ministry of the church, or try to do everything that could be done with an unspoken hope that people will appreciate how hard they are working. Meanwhile some others will do the minimum to get by and keep out of trouble.

Also influencing the parish clergy in the way they work is the fact that there will be some parishioners who want them to be a parent figure and some vicars feel or believe that is their vocation. Many clergy who do not aspire to be a parent to their congregations are aware of people who in their own sphere of work or their home life are very confident and capable but when it comes to the church they become very dependent on the clergy, even clergy who may have far less life experience or technical expertise than them. This is exemplified by the way that in many congregations if someone is taken ill people will look to the minister to take a lead in responding even though there might be a nurse or doctor in the church. The same can happen in other areas.

In the 1970s Bruce Reed argued in *The Dynamics of Religion*[2] that it was a natural and necessary process in Christian worship for people to regress into a state of dependence on another who represented God in order that they could recharge and be re-energised for their Christian work outside the church. He drew particularly on the earlier psychological theories of D. W. Winnicott who researched and wrote about the processes that help children to become mature and independent. Crucial to this was the opportunity to receive parental support and comfort in difficulty in order then to go off on their own and face new challenges. This process is seen clearly in the behaviour of a young child at a playgroup who hurts herself and comes to her mother for comfort and who is then able to get back on the play equipment again after a few minutes. This is the pattern that Reed reckoned was essential for a healthy church life, enabling church members to work out their Christian faith in the hard worlds of family, community and business life.

Whether or not it is understood in these terms many clergy feel they need to be the one who heads up the local church so that people who have various responsibilities in other spheres can have the energy and vision to carry them out. And some clergy will be reluctant to ask other people to do things because they know these others are themselves very busy. So if something needs doing they would rather do it themselves than put pressure on someone who is already committed elsewhere.

A changing climate

The situation is slowly changing. In the last two decades an increasing number of clergy have trained not in residential theological colleges but on non-residential courses, combining their studies with their often full-time jobs. Much of the tutoring on these courses is done by parish clergy and the course curriculum is in many ways rooted in the experience of local churches. This might lead to more realism amongst ordinands about what parish ministry is actually like.

In 2003 the General Synod accepted a recommendation for the reorganisation of its training of ordained ministers[3] which involved a more integrated training scheme for clergy, Readers and other lay ministers. In the long term this will change the story. No longer will people undergo a period of training at college and as a curate in order for them to go off to become the heroic and isolated parson doing the church's work. The idea of working with others will be built in from the beginning.

The church is also changing the clergy's conditions of service in order to comply with current employment legislation.[4] Until now vicars have either been appointed as incumbents with freehold or been priests-in-charge appointed for a limited period of time. Recent employment legislation is forcing a change and a new concept of common tenure might enable the church to find a way forward which is neither the absolute security regardless of performance which the freehold gives, nor the limited-term post which can no longer be enforced in law. With this proposed new concept the parish clergy would still be appointed to a particular parish, or group of parishes, and enjoy the same job security as employees in many other occupations but also, like them, be subject to capability procedures. This will mean that the clergy will have to be more adequately supervised than at present and a diocese will need to have some staff with human resources expertise. This should mean the end of a system in which vicars are appointed to their parishes and then left to do what they can even if that leads to depression, cynicism, idleness or burnout.

In 1983 the Advisory Council for the Church's Ministry published *A Strategy for the Church's Ministry* ,[5] known generally as the Tiller Report after its author John Tiller. This had two strands to it. One was that the stipendiary clergy were to become a task force for the bishop, supporting the work of local church ministry teams. The other was that local church councils and leadership groups were to be helped to identify their own particular needs and resources for ministry and the clergy's task was to help them meet their needs by a sharing of resources. This report was widely criticised and the proposals were not implemented. Some of the criticism arose from a fear that the ministry of the clergy would cease to be rooted in particular localities. Some came from those like Bruce Reed who reckoned that it was necessary for the effective functioning of the local church that there was a local priest rather than a ministry team. Many clergy were anxious that if they were part of a diocesan or area team their independence and security would be removed.

In the twenty years since then, particularly in rural areas, there has been a steady increase in the number of groups of parishes served by one vicar and in many rural as well as urban parishes there has been a development and increase in lay ministry. There are country churches where the vicar operates very much as a facilitator, assisting the local church in its work and worship and providing particular expertise when it is needed. In some places there are formal ministry teams, in others there are informal groups in which particular people are simply recognised in the local church as having certain skills and responsibilities. There are many places where the church has continued to operate effectively without one key figure on whom the members depend.

Hamley is one such place. Both the vicar and the local congregation realised that there was no way the vicar could be a parson to the parish and so church life developed in such a way that different people took on different roles. The vicar was involved in some particular pastoral situations, including funerals, weddings and baptisms, provided training and support, she led study courses, had an overall management

129

brief and twice a month led the worship. Most other things were done by local church members including leading many other services. The meeting described earlier was a group of people who had each taken on a small section of the parish to be a church contact there, keeping people in touch with each other and with the church and speaking to the vicar of any who they felt particularly needed a visit from the clergy for some reason.

In describing the reactions to his proposals Tiller spoke of the Church of England as having a 'dynamic conservatism',[6] a way of summoning up enormous energy to avoid having to change. But it has changed, albeit rather slowly. It has changed more in some places than others and the change has been piecemeal and sometimes reactive rather than overall and strategic. But whilst there are some who remember or dream of the days of the parson in the parish there is a much greater acceptance now in country parishes that in the future things will have to be done differently. There is also often a sense that alternative ways of being a church are not something to be adopted reluctantly because the old way is no longer practically possible, but that new ways are in some respects better.

The country parson approach to rural ministry is defunct. However it works out in detail, the alternative is going to involve members of the local church working together. They might simply work together in order to support the local vicar because the vicar cannot manage on his or her own. But they might recognise themselves as the local church with the vicar there as someone who can support them and work with them. And there is no reason why the good features of Herbert's model cannot be characteristics of a new way of working.

The Magazine

The Archdeacon had picked up the magazine as he came into the church. Sometimes they really didn't look like something you wanted to read but this one was attractive. It was well presented and had a photograph of people on the cover. He'd had a few minutes to spare before the service began so had browsed through it. Inside there were details of what was going on in the parishes: Lent lunches, advance notice of Christian Aid week, and a few extracts of a letter from Nepal.

There was information about services and a report of the Christingle at Nebthorne Briars. They were running a Lent course using a book by the Archbishop. There was an advert for a diocesan training day on listening skills and a retreat at Polwell House.

And if anyone couldn't get to church and wanted communion at home they should contact the Reader. Someone else was co-ordinating a car scheme to the doctor's in Betterly.

There was no vicar's letter because there was no vicar. That's why he was there. There had been a vacancy for eight months now. The parishes' advert in the Church Times *had elicited five expressions of interest and two applicants, both of whom seemed to think moving from suburbia to the country would be like an early retirement. The churchwardens had asked him to scout around a bit before they advertised again.*

The magazine had an editorial instead, which was fairly upbeat about church life even though the wardens and others were disappointed there was no sign of a vicar. One of the churchwardens, Mary Blackford, came into the vestry.

'Is everything OK?' she said.

'Fine thanks. I was looking at your magazine. It seems as if you're doing everything, anyway. Why do you want a vicar?'

She thought for a moment, then said, 'To help us do it better.'

8

Working It Out Together

The church for the world

Archbishop William Temple is reputed to have said that the church exists for the benefit of those outside it. The point can be made a number of ways. John's gospel talks about Jesus coming so people can have life, and have it abundantly (John 10:10). In the first three gospels, the synoptic gospels, Jesus talks a little about the church but a great deal about the kingdom of God. Bruce Reed, in *The Dynamics of Religion*, warned about ecclesiasticism, a dysfunctional form of religion in which people are preoccupied with the church and its affairs rather than able to leave the church's worship energised for engagement with the things of God in the world.[1]

There is a danger that as church members take greater responsibility for the life of the local church they will be distracted from their prime task which is living out the Christian faith in their work and their communities. However, this does not necessarily follow. The kind of preoccupation that Reed talks about does not come from people having responsibility for the life of the church but from their needing to emotionally stay around the church for assurance and comfort, like children who are unable to leave their parents to play with others on the swings. Taking some responsibility for the church's life is a matter of growing up as a Christian.

Any local church has a number of tasks that need to be done for it to function properly. Some of those tasks will go with official roles, such as churchwarden, musician, children's worker or treasurer. Others will be less obvious roles, such as the unselfconscious care for neighbours which church members often practise within their communities. Others will be practical jobs that people need to take on, like arranging flowers, cleaning, cutting grass, routine building maintenance, organising social events, providing transport for people who are not very mobile, and so on.

If things need doing people need to do them. Ideally there will be some members of a local church who will have time to do them while others will not. Many country clergy will be aware of one or two people in their churches who would be excellent churchwardens but they do not have the time, because much of the spare time they have is given to other very worthwhile activities, in local government, health trusts, housing trusts, charitable organisations, and other things which are all part of the work of God in the world. There are other people whose work is such that they need to be able to come to church without any sense of responsibility for its organisation but as a place to relax and recharge their batteries.

In reality it is sometimes people who do not have a great deal of time who struggle to do what is necessary for the running of the church. That can be hard, particularly if there seem to be other church members who are unable or unwilling to do things themselves but are very willing to criticise others for not doing them properly. Or people who would be willing to take on some of these things but would make other people's lives a misery by their attitude or words if they did. Or if there are people in the local community who contribute little to the church's life but are willing to voice an opinion about poor standards.

Sometimes in a country parish it is very difficult to find people who will take on particular responsibilities. This can be the case in a very lively church as well as one where not much seems to happen. The problem sometimes is that all the likely people are either already fully committed to other valuable things or have done their time and are now retired to a less active style of church membership. But people need to take things on for the church to function. Sometimes it will fall to the vicar in his or her role as manager to try to find people to take on key tasks but at other times local church members will do it. Much depends on the situation.

Together with finding people to take on tasks and roles goes the job of making clear what is actually involved. Sometimes this is no problem. Someone taking on the flower rota will probably do exactly what their predecessor did. Sidesmen or stewards can be told what is required by those already doing it or by churchwardens. But the church-wardens' job is less well defined, being, like the vicar's job, something that has developed and changed over the years.[2] Every situation is different. Every church in a cluster of parishes will be composed of people with different gifts and personalities and will have its customs and practices which vary. And all of this will change over time as different people take on the different tasks that need to be done.

Deciding how to do the job

Within all this vicars need some way of deciding what they give time and attention to. Some won't want to think about it, they'll just want to get on with the job. This might mean they will do what they have always done, or that they will do what they like doing, or they'll do what seems necessary to stop themselves feeling guilty, or they will obey Whinger's Law which states that those who make the most fuss get their own way and so they will respond to those who are making the loudest demands at any particular moment. Others will want to reflect on what they are doing, with the belief that by standing back for a short while and thinking what they are doing and why they are doing it they might be able to do things better for God, for their parishioners and for themselves. Ideally they will do this with the leaders of the local churches.

Simply prioritising jobs is valuable. Many vicars find that every day they are listing tasks and setting them in order of importance, possibly on paper but maybe just in their heads. And as the day goes on things change and they have to weigh up and rejig their mental list. The morning's work was clear but something else arises, a visit must be made urgently, an e-mail needs speedy attention and a little research, or they remember that the deadline for an article or a service plan was that very day and everything has to be reordered. But the more basic question is what should be on the list in the first place. What actually is the vicar's job?

It is possible to draw up a job description and it has been done. The statements that are found in the canons of the church or the ordination service are far too general to be of much use in working out what the vicar must do in a particular parish.[3] They sketch out a picture of a vicar working in the impossible parson mode. But from the Church Representation Rules it is possible to draw up an outline for a PCC's responsibilities. From this a vicar and churchwardens can decide their particular areas of responsibility, which will often be the churchwardens taking responsibility for matters to do with buildings and finance and the vicar taking the rest. By a process of elimination this leaves the vicar with an outline job description. But again it is very broad, and any statement which moves from saying that the vicar will endeavour to do particular things to saying this is what the vicar will do is likely to be a recipe for a breakdown. A job description might provide a map of the territory but it does not necessarily help the vicar navigate through it.

It is more helpful to work out which roles are the most important ones for the vicar to take and which can be neglected or only taken up when essential. Thinking in terms of roles moves attention from particular tasks but enables a person to think what kind of work they might be doing and how they might approach it. A vicar can list in order of priority the different possible roles he or she could take in a parish, bearing in mind how things are in that place, who else among the church members has the time and the skills to do particular things, how the church relates to the community as a whole, and how things might develop in the future. And a vicar can often discuss this with the local church.

There are a number of ways this can be done. The discussion might be with a PCC or with a group of churchwardens, or perhaps with another small group of church members. It can begin with the vicar or maybe someone else outlining the vicar's possible roles. Any list that is presented can be compared with people's initial expectations of what the vicar might do, what has been expected in the past, what other people in the parish might expect and how realistic these expectations are. There can be discussion about the state and priorities of the church and the needs of the parish.

Then, at some point the group together needs to decide which roles they think are most important for the vicar in their particular place. This might emerge quite simply but sometimes it might take some teasing out. One way of doing this is with a ballot paper exercise. Each person has a paper which lists the possibilities, maybe the twelve roles listed in chapter six; maybe another list. Each person then numbers them in order of priority, number one going to the highest priority, with no one being allowed to give the same number to two different roles. The results are then added up and the role which has the overall lowest score is the one which has the highest priority in the group's view.

This prioritising might then need to be discussed further if members of the group disagree sharply and there is no consensus, or they see that different roles given a high priority will create a tension for the vicar. Or if the group's view is very different from the vicar's own. Listing these possible roles and having to decide between them helps a group think how feasible or how impossible it is for one person to undertake them all.

Everyone, including the vicar, needs to be aware that even when a clear picture has emerged there will be many occasions when, for a period, the order of priority changes. A vicar who in one place might clearly need to work as a teacher within the church might still for some time have to put that aside in order to devote time to pastoral work or to management. This will happen because of crises. It will also happen through the seasons. Christmas, for instance, is thought by many people to be the vicar's busy time because they are very visible, taking services and doing home visits. There is certainly plenty to do at Christmas but other things can be deferred. No one wants church council meetings over Christmas and there is no point trying to deal with much administrative work because people either do not want to know or they are not in their offices. In March vicars are much less visible but might have more to do, particularly if they are running a Lent course, preparing for Easter services and also getting ready for a round of Annual Parochial Church Meetings, all of which have to be held before the end of April and will include the receiving of reports and the appointment of church officers in every parish.

Working out overall priorities gives a general sense of direction for the vicar. It does not determine what the vicar does every day or even every week. Making the day-to-day decisions is like navigating through a rocky strait. You go straight ahead by continually changing direction. Some vicars can think in terms of short-term, medium-term and long-term priorities. The overall long-term priority for the vicar might be to work on helping a local church in its Christian discipleship, but in the medium term the vicar might have to operate in a chaplaincy mode, engaging with the wider community in which the local church is set. In the very short term, however, the vicar might be stuck behind a desk clearing some essential paperwork.

What is important is also not necessarily what takes the most time and energy. This is true of many areas of work. A builder may spend a lot of time in preparing tenders and dealing with suppliers though the important work is the actual construction. A teacher will spend time preparing lessons, marking and keeping records while they are quite clear that it is the actual contact time with the students that matters. It can help the frustrated builder or teacher if they can see this other work as important for achieving the overall aim. But there will also be distractions. The builder will have to deal with equipment breakdowns, disagreements among the workforce, illness and unexpected discoveries on the site, not to speak of design errors, delayed deliveries and unsatisfactory staff. The teacher has to deal with classroom discipline, firedrills, absenteeism and emotional and relationship problems among the students. This is life and vicars cannot expect to always be able to operate in the roles which they and others believe to be most important.

The vicar and other ministers

The roles of the vicar will need to be worked out together with an exploration of the possible roles of other church ministers. It may be that a meeting of churchwardens or a PCC cannot do this but that the vicar needs to do this separately with any Readers, non-stipendiary ministers, active retired clergy or other local ministers. It may be that they form a local ministry team which meets regularly and can occasionally take some time out to stand back and assess what each one is doing, what roles each one takes in the parishes where they work, and whether or not that should be changed or adjusted. It may be that the vicar needs to do this on a one-to-one basis as a form of ministry review for each of these lay or ordained ministers. They each have their particular strengths and gifts and also things they are not so good at. The vicar will need to work with this in the same way that the vicar works with the gifts and resources of each local congregation.

In many industrial or business situations a team will be formed deliberately ensuring that people with different personalities are a part, all bringing their different gifts and able to play to their strengths, at least in theory. In a voluntary organisation like the church that is much less likely to happen. Jesus may have picked his team but not many vicars can pick theirs. The local church is a self-selecting group. The PCC is their representatives who have all volunteered or at least been persuaded to take on the task. They might be the only people willing and able to do so. The likelihood of a wide range of complementary skills being present in a country church council is quite remote. There will be large gaps. Vicars sometimes have to take on roles for which they are not well suited but which are necessary. They have to be the person of vision and ideas when they would much rather follow someone else's lead. They have to get up front, giving thanks, boosting morale, and speaking on behalf of the church, when they would much rather talk or listen in a corner. They have to spend time at a desk when they would much rather be out and about in the parishes but they know that if this crucial piece of organisation was not done by them then a lot of other important things would not happen either.

Sometimes the vicar needs to stand back in order that other ministers can play to their own strengths or through practice develop particular skills. A Reader may need to be given opportunities to preach on occasions when the vicar would like to do it but the Reader needs the experience or needs to be given opportunities to take on this very visible role in the church in order that their other church work is strengthened, perhaps their visiting or other pastoral work. And sometimes the other members of the local church will need to have someone other than the vicar doing what they have perhaps previously thought of as the vicar's work not only because the vicar cannot do it but because this person can and needs to be given the opportunity. And sometimes the other person will be better at it than the vicar.

In a discussion about the vicar's work with churchwardens or a PCC it might become clear that the local church places a high priority on something which the vicar finds extremely difficult. In that case the question is either how can the local church help the vicar, or is there someone else who should take on this role? Sometimes there will be such a person and a Reader, a retired vicar, a non-stipendiary minister, a churchwarden or another lay church member might then fulfil a role in a community which previously the locals had always thought must be the vicar's.

Different roles in different parishes

Often the roles that a vicar needs to take on in one parish will be different from those in another, and the vicar will need to take on different roles again with regard to the whole group of parishes in which he or she works. It may well be that the whole group of parishes needs a vicar who will take on a management role, organising who will take services week by week, finding people willing to be church officers, and steering a benefice council or churchwardens' meeting through the stormy waters of sharing the working expenses, settling the Christmas service plan and deciding whether a particular parishioner should be able to train as a Reader. But in some of those individual parishes they can perhaps manage their own affairs. A churchwarden, secretary or a PCC Vice-Chair might be better than the vicar at organising events and handling disgruntled parishioners. They might not only have more skill but also the local knowledge and form.

Elsewhere a group of parishes might not need a vicar to manage their affairs. There may be among the church members someone who is very skilled in helping a group of local church leaders work together and develop their church life. Such a person may have already helped the parishes through a vacancy, when perhaps for eighteen months they were without a vicar, and now they have one there are other things they want the vicar to do. It may be pastoral work or perhaps the worship needs attention across the group or maybe the local schools need time from the vicar, as a governor or in support for the teachers with worship and RE.

But while the vicar may need to take on particular key roles with regard to a whole group of parishes, in each particular parish different roles might be needed. In one parish, because of some local problems or the way the church's ministry has been in recent years, the vicar may need to allocate time to calling on people simply to make contact, listen and help people be aware that the church cares about them. But in another parish local people might be able to do that either formally visiting or through their social networks. In that place they might need someone who will help them develop services for special occasions involving a small group of young people. Meanwhile another parish may have serious divisions over the proposed development of a quarry and the vicar may need to visit, attend meetings, and help both sides hear each other and acknowledge the value of both preserving the environment and providing local employment. Or there may be agitation and campaigning about a camp for asylum seekers or New Age travellers and the vicar might need to be involved in the debates, contributing as well as listening. In another parish the church members might simply be tired or stale and need encouragement to think, to dream and imagine, and be given a vision of what their church might become.

Difficulties with discussing the vicar's work

Some vicars will feel and believe that they on their own are the people to decide what their principal roles should be. They have their theological insight which they have developed over the years, perhaps including an understanding of the psychology and sociology of small communities. They have their past experience of parish ministry, which may be extensive. Being in some ways apart from the local community, by their ordination and their having come from elsewhere, they perhaps feel they can see more clearly than anyone else what is going on in the parishes.

They may have come with a clear vision of what is needed generally in the country church. They may have been specifically asked by the bishop to take charge of the parish because he believes this priest has gifts and skills which the local church needs to take it through a crisis or beyond a division. Even without such an episcopal directive a vicar might feel that having been appointed by the bishop or by God he is going to decide for himself, perhaps with the bishop's or God's help, how he goes about his work. Or a vicar might feel that she has enough to contend with in this place with various commitments and numerous demands without having other people tell her how to do this job. Sometimes a vicar's level of stress or anxiety is such that they cannot face the thought of trying to discuss their work with anyone, let alone the churchwardens or a PCC.

But even if vicars want to discuss their work with their local church leaders it can sometimes be difficult. It may be that the church members have earlier made it quite clear that they have an expectation of the vicar which the vicar cannot possibly fulfil and they will not talk about it further. Perhaps they cannot get their minds around what it might mean for a vicar to have four or more parishes and can only imagine their vicar doing what the vicar of forty years ago did. It may be that they have had a bad experience, perhaps of a vicar in the past who did very little, and they assume that any discussion about what the vicar might do is an attempt by the vicar to get out of what they see as the vicar's job.

In some rural congregations it is very hard to find out the views of more than one person. That person might be the local landowner or the landowner's agent who has run the village and the church for many years, and the congregation, being also tenants and employees, are not given to disagreeing with the landowner. The person may be someone who has kept the church going for many years and other church members are very aware of this, perhaps regularly reminded of the fact, and do not want to upset them by disagreeing. Sometimes that one person may be someone who has lived in the village for a while and has employed in this small congregation all the skills they developed and used before their retirement to become a big fish in a much bigger pool and who now treats the church as their personal fief. The person may speak from such a depth of experience and with such erudition that no one else feels able to contribute anything worth saying. Or the person may simply be a bully that no one else will stand up to.

It is part of the myth of rural England that villages are jolly places where everyone mucks in together. In reality they can be boards on which people play out all sorts of power games. They are locations in which people of very different personalities meet and those meetings are not always comfortable for all concerned.

Small communities work in very different ways from large ones. In a large community, a big town or city suburb, people will generally only meet when they arrange to. They meet at clubs and societies, evening classes, pubs and churches. The likelihood is that between one meeting and the next they will have little to do with each other unless they choose to. In traditional settled communities it is possible for people to meet several times a day, and for the people they meet in the pub or the church to be the same people as they work with and who are also possibly their relatives. The way that traditional societies in many parts of England have dealt with this is by people 'keeping their heads down'. They keep their thoughts, feelings and opinions to themselves. A dispute in one place can spill over into many others so is best avoided. If you make yourself vulnerable to one group of people you are vulnerable everywhere so people keep themselves to themselves and may find it hard to express their views even if they want to. In other rural subcultures people deal with this interconnectedness in the opposite way, with a speak-as-I-find style which intimidates newcomers until they learn to respond in kind.

It may be that members of a congregation, be they churchwardens or members of a church council, do not want to be suggesting to their vicar how he or she should spend their time. Maybe they would rather not think about it. Maybe they respect totally the vicar's own judgement. Far be it from them to tell the vicar what to do. Unfortunately such a reluctance does not always mean they will not complain later if the vicar has got it wrong. It might be that the lay church members are short-sighted and think that if everyone just carries on as they always have done everything will be all right. Or they might be selfish, not concerned for the other churches in their group, let alone in the diocese and the wider world. Or they may only be concerned about themselves, the church, and not about other parishioners.

A great deal of work has been done in recent decades on collaborative workstyles, both beyond and within the church.[4] Working together can mean a number of different things. It can mean two or more people working on the same task, a group deciding together on how to go about a project and then sharing out the different jobs that need doing to complete it, or several people sharing resources and discussing their work as they find helpful or necessary. Different approaches are appropriate for different situations. A squad repairing a water main, a team developing and building a ticket machine and the doctors in a health centre all work together, but in very different ways. Within a group of churches the vicar, in the role of manager, will need to help the members of the churches work together. Sometimes this will involve thinking out, perhaps with the church members, which are the most appropriate ways of doing so.

While there is a lot that can steer country vicars towards deciding on their own what principal roles they need to adopt within their parishes and how they ought to spend their time and their energy, this is far from ideal. A vicar can assess the needs of a particular parish but so too can the locals. They have their own view of how things are, they know the history, they know some of the people better than the vicar ever will. The vicar brings freshness and theological expertise, perhaps experience of other parishes, and insights from the wider church. The lay church members may also have some of these. They also have their own local knowledge. Pooling their insights they can possibly work out better what is needed than the vicar can alone.

Vicars will need to be aware that the lay church members' assessment of the parish's needs are no more objective than their own. The vicar's theological perspective is going to be influenced to some extent by the vicar's own personality. Vicars also have their own enthusiasms. Those who like teaching will see a need for it. Those who like music might also see it as very important. Those who do not like to be under pressure are more likely to want to develop a 'ministry of being' with a leisured lifestyle which they can then justify on theological grounds.

Lay church members, being just as human as vicars are, can do the same thing. They too have their preferences and their vested interests. They might think it essential that the vicar goes around the parish visiting all the elderly people, which is something which they could do but do not want to do. They might consider it most important that the vicar takes responsibility for locking and unlocking the church every day, and thus relieves them of the responsibility of doing it. Or the PCC Secretary might firmly believe that all letters from the church should come from the vicar, thereby relieving him of a certain amount of unexciting work.

There are those who actually want to be a holy remnant, a faithful few who are maintaining the church in a time of neglect and religious apathy. So they do not really want there to be more people involved in the church's life, although they would not admit it to themselves, let alone to others. Some want others involved but only on their terms, keeping things the way they like, thereby reinforcing their sense that the way they do them is the right way while also relieving them of some of the effort involved in changing things. The vicar might need to be alert to some of the little power games that can go on in small communities and small churches as well as large.

Nevertheless, the vicar is a member of such a church with all its failings. Together this little section of frail humanity is to do God's work in the parish. People have different experiences and different insights into how this can best be done. The vicar has an important contribution to make but needs to work with the local church not only in the task but in working out what the task is, and in working out the vicar's part in it.

The vicar in three dimensions

Some PCCs develop a mission statement which says succinctly what they are about. Some will go further down this road and set themselves targets. Many will baulk at this kind of business-world ethos, including many who earn their living there. They want the church to be a different kind of world. But however they do it there must be some value in a church council from time to time taking stock of its church life and talking over what it needs to be doing, beyond the next building repair and the harvest festival. The question of what roles the vicar is to take can follow on from that. What is needed of the vicar to help the church move forward?

One dimension of a church's life is its worship and prayer and some churches, when they think of how their life should develop, are aware of the need for change in this area. It may be a change of style, as in the developing of new forms of service for a new constituency, be it young families or older people who have perhaps been marginalised by the church's practice in previous years. But it may be an increased depth that is needed. In the role of liturgist, priest or pastor the vicar is working particularly in this dimension. The liturgist develops the forms of service. The priest is a leader of worship, be it in the Sunday Eucharist or praying at the bedside of a sick person. The pastor is concerned that people grow spiritually, perhaps in releasing aspects of their humanity or maybe in their personal prayer life.

In the roles of church representative, chaplain and social activist the vicar is more directed towards the church's community life. As the representative the vicar becomes the public face of the church, whether it be giving thanks to the workers at the annual fete or speaking to the press about a local crisis. As a chaplain the vicar is a community theologian and on occasion an advocate for a neglected group within the community or a mediator between factions. The social activist is concerned not just to serve society but to change it, perhaps leading a campaign to improve life for some members of the local community or reminding a village community that it is part of a much wider humanity that all matters to God.

The evangelist is concerned to bring people of little faith into a greater trust in God and deeper commitment to Christ. The teacher is concerned to help them learn from Christ, through the Bible, through the wisdom of the church, and from the Spirit of God through their own experience. The focus for lifestylers is their own discipleship: to be true to what God is calling them to be in that particular place.

But the manager, the administrator and the leader are operating much more as resources for the local church. The manager's concern is the church's human resources. The manager wants the church's members to be working together and working well. The administrator wants to get practical things done which will enable this to happen. The leader's concern is that the church together has a vision of where it should be going and where it could be.

Within these different dimensions of a local church's life the vicar may need to take a pivotal position, heading up the work or providing crucial resources to others. It may be that other church members can do this and what is needed of the vicar is to fill in some spaces. There may be a church which is well able to develop its worship towards meeting the needs of the local community. There may be a Reader and other lay members with significant gifts in this area. That church may need the vicar to focus on the community dimension of the church's life, helping people who are already members get to know each other, or maybe being the front person or a chaplain in a parish where few of the church members have the time or the opportunity to meet up with their neighbours. Or it may be that the active church members are already well enmeshed with their local community but need the vicar to focus on helping them learn and become more confident in their faith.

Releasing the vicar

Vicars have to respond to the demands of parish ministry moment by moment, managing their diaries and working out their short-term priorities, but they can often do this within a wider framework which comes from a discussion with the leadership of the local churches about what is needed in which place. Doing it within this framework can release them from a sense or a feeling that they need to do everything. People can affirm them in what they are doing. A vicar might be encouraged to do something which she would like to do but can so easily neglect with a misguided sense of urgency about other matters. Many people want their vicar to be someone who is informed about the world and who can relate the Bible and Christian theology to the things that matter to them, but many clergy will neglect the necessary study because they feel they need to be visible about the parish all the time. Most people want to know what is going on in their local church and what they are expected to do to help it happen, yet many clergy neglect basic administration because they feel that this is not proper ministry. People also

148

usually want their church services to be taken seriously, but for many parish clergy there is a temptation to come to Sunday worship badly prepared because other things seemed much more important than setting aside the necessary time. Many people probably want their vicar to be someone who prays for them although the vicar might feel uncomfortable spending time in the church at prayer when other people their age are at work. Bringing other people into this discussion about priorities and roles can sometimes release the clergy from unrealistic ideas of what others expect or want. It can also give the parish clergy support in maintaining their priorities.

A church member visits an elderly neighbour.

'I don't see the vicar much now. Haven't seen him for years.' It is not an unusual comment and the visitor can respond in several ways. For example: 'I know. It's a shame isn't it.' This confirms the condemnation of the vicar for failing in the task of visiting.

But the visitor could respond, 'Well, he does have five parishes to get round now.' This elicits pity for the vicar and suggests that the unvisited parishioner is just not important enough to come to the vicar's attention.

But the visitor could say something along the lines of, 'I know. The PCC have asked the vicar in this parish to focus particularly on developing study groups and preparing our new service books, so they have asked me to call and see you instead.' That may not provide total satisfaction for the parishioner but it does flag up that this is a joint enterprise and the parishioner is not unimportant. If the vicar is able to talk out with the local church leaders how he or she will go about their work the other church leaders are able to provide support for the vicar, whether that be affirming them in what they are doing, offering information and advice about local situations, or watching the vicar's back.

Rooting the vicar's ministry

Discussion of the vicar's work with the local church leaders also helps to root the vicar's ministry in the particular place.

This was one of the great values of Herbert's country parson. He was not simply like an eighteenth-century flying curate, dashing in to take a service then rushing on to the next place, or like a medieval hedge priest, hired to perform the necessary religious function and then dismissed and travelling on to another place. Herbert's parson belonged somewhere and present-day vicars who work out their priorities and approaches together with the local church leadership are going to root their ministries in their particular communities.

The ministry of Herbert's country parson was also to both individual people and to the community of which he was a part. A country vicar working alone can try to relate to both, and might succeed. Working with lay church members the vicar will be part of the church community within the wider parish community and may be better able to respond to the needs of that whole community as well as to individual parishioners in need. The vicar can work with the local church leadership in developing a response to the local community's needs and within that response the vicar will have a part alongside others.

The Share

It often happened that way. It was while he was driving home that he thought of what he should have said. And then it was too late.

Archdeacon Richard Cutter had been at Holdall, a commuter village some twelve miles from Dorminster. The rural dean had suggested he meet with the PCC as they had said they wouldn't pay their parish share this year and he had felt that the Archdeacon would be a better person to persuade them.

Visiting an unknown PCC, of course, he did not know the members, but it was an interesting diversion to try to guess their occupations and backgrounds from occasional clues. Three of the men appeared to have their own businesses, and one was probably ex-military. One of the women was a farmer's wife, another was a primary-school teacher, and he thought a third was possibly some kind of therapist. But the treasurer, the new treasurer, was a bank manager. And it seemed he was taking the PCC with him.

They were not without money, even in their church account. But they wanted to keep thirty thousand pounds as a contingency fund. They didn't know what for and they realised that if they suddenly needed money for the building they could probably raise it in an appeal. Many of the parishioners who never came to church would contribute to keep the roof on and the church open.

The PCC also argued that they shouldn't have to pay because they didn't have a vicar. Their previous vicar had left seven months ago. Their group of three parishes was joining with two from a neighbouring group and that had taken time to sort out. The living was suspended and as yet the Archdeacon had not been able to find someone for the bishop to appoint as priest-in-charge.

'So,' they said, 'why should we pay our parish share when we don't have a vicar?'

'Because the parish share is not to pay your vicar. It's your contribution to the diocesan funds which are needed to pay all the clergy in the diocese.'

'So let the parishes that have vicars contribute to the cost of them.'

'But you are part of the diocese as well.'

'But we don't get anything out of it.'

'You do. You have the support of a Rural Dean, you can draw on the resources of the training department and others, the diocese contributes to the expenses of your visiting clergy and there are people in the administration doing the work so that another vicar can be appointed.

'But it's not about paying for what we get. It is about working together and sharing resources. If you were a congregational church you would only pay for your own minister and a small amount to the association. But we're not a congregational church. We are an episcopal church. You are part of a bigger unit, the diocese, and in that we support each other.'

'But what would happen if we didn't pay?'

'I wouldn't send round the bailiffs and there wouldn't be a ceremonial cursing at the cathedral! We would carry on providing what support we can and trying to find you another parish priest, but we'd do it knowing that you are acting as if you are not part of the organisation we belong to. And other parishes would have to pay more.'

'Not much. Our share spread among all the parishes in the diocese would not cost them each much more.'

'No, but some of them are other parishes who also don't have a vicar and they are contributing. And some of them are places where no one in the congregation has anything at all in the bank. They live on their wages or a giro and those that owe money don't owe it to Visa but to some loan shark. But together they still manage to pay a parish share.'

'But surely, if there are places without vicars,' said the teacher, 'then the diocese needs less money.'

'No, because the diocesan budget is worked out on the basis that *there will always be a certain number of vacancies. There always are. It's just a matter of where they are going to be. At the moment you are among the fifty or so parishes without a parish priest.'*

And so it went on but eventually he'd said, 'You've got a choice. You can either contribute your parish share and act as if you're part of the diocese, or keep your money in the bank and act as if you're not.'

That was the bit he'd thought about afterwards. After further argument and a vote they did agree to pay. But what he realised he could have said was that they had a third possibility. They could have paid their parish share and rather than keep the remainder to help themselves another day they could give away the rest of their reserve to Christian Aid and help people who need it now.

But, as usual, he thought of that too late.

9

Bigger Circles

The vicar and the diocese

At a licensing or induction service the bishop or his representative says to the vicar, 'Receive the care of souls which is both mine and yours.' It is quite possible that the vicar will not actually see the diocesan bishop again for several years but there is an important point here about the nature of the Anglican Church. The vicar is working as a priest within a diocese and not just as a local minister. Even if there is little actual contact with the bishop the vicar will receive communications from the diocesan office, will be able to make use of the resources of the diocese, and will receive a stipend from the Church Commissioners whose money comes from the diocese. Each year the vicar will need to attend an archdeacon's visitation and it is likely that the vicar will have other contact with the archdeacon during the year.

There may be a diocesan policy for ministry development and for mission. The cluster of parishes in which a vicar works may have been formed as part of a diocesan strategy or it may have been an ad hoc arrangement, simply putting together vacant benefices as they became available. But the nature of any possible local ministry team will certainly be influenced by diocesan policy. Some dioceses now have locally ordained ministers, others do not. Some take on a large number of retired or self-employed clergy in house-for-duty posts, others do not. Some train and license Readers simply with a view to them conducting services and preaching while others expect Readers to specialise in teaching or pastoral work as well as leading worship. Some dioceses have autho-rised lay pastoral assistants, others do not. In some dioceses experiments in lay ministry are encouraged, whereas in others the bishop and other leaders are quite strict about keeping to the rules. All these will influence the way that a vicar can work with and develop the churches' ministry within a group of parishes.

The diocese will also have resources on which the vicar can call. There will be diocesan staff who are specialists in partic-ular areas of work and whose task is to support the local churches in children's and youth work, issues of social responsibility, communications, rural issues, mission and evangelism, ecumenical relations, inter-faith matters, racial justice, health and healing, pastoral care and counselling, and other areas. Every diocese has a Board of Education which has responsibility for supporting church schools. These resources are not just for the local clergy but for the churches, and vicars can recommend to other church members that they contact the relevant diocesan officer for advice on a particular matter.

Every diocese will also have some staff who are responsible for the in-service training of clergy and the teaching and training of all other church members. Such training provision often consists of courses which the parish clergy can choose to attend to enhance their skills or to develop their theology and spirituality and their understanding of church and society. The Church of England's 2001 policy document *Mind the Gap* envisaged continuing ministerial education as being 'to equip and develop the Church's ministers in order that they may stimulate and enable the whole Church to partici-pate more fully in the mission of God in the world'.[1] Significantly this is referring not just to the in-service training of clergy but the continuing education of all ministers, lay and ordained. The document provided a framework for relating the provision of continuing education to the needs of the ministers as perceived in the ongoing review of their work. Sometimes in a local church the vicar can be left to work at what he or she is good at but often vicars must take on roles and tasks which do not come easily to them. And even where clergy do not need to develop new skills they need to improve the ones they have and to develop their understanding and their theological insight.

But if vicars are to plan their work with their local church leaders they will sometimes need support in that as well. Taking seriously the need for parish clergy to work out their priorities with their local churches will mean training departments also operating in a consultancy mode. This does not mean one training officer trying to be a consultant to two hundred vicars and their PCCs but it will mean training departments developing the consultancy skills of lay church members and clergy so that they can help each other in this process, or identifying people within the diocese who already have these skills and helping them work at this task.

Bishops and archdeacons can also help. Archdeacons meet with their churchwardens once a year at the Archdeacon's Visitation. It is possible for an archdeacon at such a gathering to stimulate thought and discussion by encouraging churchwardens to think about what it is reasonable to expect of the parish clergy and by giving some pointers as to how they can work together efficiently. Archdeacons are also involved in the appointments of vicars and the period when an archdeacon and a local church are looking for a new vicar is a good time for exploring what the new vicar might be expected to do. Most parishes want a young vicar, married with children who will attend the local school, and energetic, good with young people but able to make time for the elderly as well, and who will lead the church forward into a period of spiritual and numerical growth while maintaining the old traditions. But most parishes are not going to get this, and they know it. It is a shame if the PCC or group of churchwardens do not talk further and try to explore what roles they actually want a new vicar to take on, aware that the new vicar cannot do everything. Such a conversation might also help them see more of what they can do for themselves. And it might mean that when a likely candidate comes along they are able to have a realistic conversation about what this

person might do. An archdeacon, the rural dean or a consultant can help in this process by earthing it in the realm of the
possible.

Even when they have worked on from an unrealistic hope
a group of parishes is still not likely to get exactly what they
want in their new vicar. Parishes sometimes go for very long
periods without a vicar, relying on the services of retired
clergy and Readers, with lay members doing many of the
essential tasks which previous vicars have done and relying
on the rural dean as a backstop in crises or for advice, and
they sometimes get to the point where they just want anyone
who will come. But if the local church has begun this kind of
thinking about a vicar's possible roles they are better placed
to be able to work out a realistic idea of what an actual vicar
can do. Then when a person does come and has become
familiar with the parishes they can work out together what in
those parishes are the most important roles for the vicar to
take.

Some adjustment of ideas might be needed. A parish might
have initially hoped for someone who would principally be a
pastor and whilst the new vicar could spend a lot of time calling on people around the parishes they might in time realise
that the vicar would do better helping the local churches do
this. Or perhaps they had hoped for someone with imagination and vision who would help them and encourage them
after a dry and difficult period but the new vicar might be
better at listening quietly and exploring with them their own
hopes for the church and their own spiritual lives. Perhaps
they wanted someone who would go out and encourage new
people to come to church but they realise after a while that
what this person can do, and is likely to do instead, is help
them pray and worship God in a way that is much deeper
than their previous simple faithful attendance. Maybe church
membership will follow from this. Maybe it won't. Maybe
that is God's problem and their business is simply to be more
in touch with God.

Induction services are an opportunity for a bishop to speak
about what can and cannot be expected of the new vicar. It is

quite possible that the bishop has very little first-hand experience of being a vicar, and even if he has some experience he has not been the vicar of these parishes at this time. But if before the appointment the PCCs have thought of what they were looking for from their new vicar this information should be available to the bishop. Many of the congregation at an induction service will have a very vague notion of what it is that vicars do anyway and any clarification of this will help the new vicar.

The development of any diocesan strategy for ministry development needs to be a two-way process, a conversation or discussion. Those who have an overview of the diocese, the bishops, archdeacons and diocesan officers, only know what it is like on the ground if they listen to the parish clergy and members of local churches. The diocesan staff need to plan for the diocese drawing on their own theological insights and previous experience, but they also need to draw on the insights and experience of the locals. This can be done using the synods, pastoral committees at different levels in a diocese – the deanery, archdeaconry and whole diocese – and by separate consultations. It is quite possible for a bishop to decide that he will not introduce locally ordained ministry, or that he will authorise some people as lay pastoral assistants, or that clusters of parishes should be made into single parish units, or that the clergy in a rural area should be based in the towns and go out to the villages without exploring with local churches and their clergy whether, on the basis of their thinking and experience, these are a good thing. But it would be foolish. It would fail to respect the fact that other members of the community of Christians have valuable insights drawn from their varied experiences. Obviously not everyone can be consulted about everything but the Church of England as it is constituted already has representative structures and it makes sense for these to be used.

There have been suggestions in the past, particularly by Leslie Paul in 1964[2] and to some extent by John Tiller in 1983,[3] that the parish clergy should become part of a diocesan workforce. This has been fiercely resisted for a number of reasons, not least the fact that it runs counter to the parson concept of the vicar. But even though the parson model is now obsolete there is still good reason for not having the stipendiary clergy as diocesan rather than parish priests. Even if the stipendiary clergy now have several parishes they are still rooted in that locality and will develop local knowledge. Their knowledge can then be fed into the development of a diocesan strategy, either through a process of consultation or through the simple fact that they will work out any strategy with regard to what is feasible within their parishes. A team of clergy as a diocesan workforce could easily lose that connection with the church on the ground.

At the same time it is important the clergy do not become buried in their parishes but are able to contribute to local church life a wider view of what the church is about. Whilst having their feet on the ground of a particular place they need to have a wide view, and this can come partly from being in touch with the life of the wider church of the diocese and beyond. John Wesley's catchphrase was that the world was his parish. There is always a danger that for country clergy the parish can be their world and this should be avoided.

Local support

It was to try to help the clergy have a wider perspective that deanery chapters were developed in the nineteenth century. The deanery is the grouping of parishes between the benefice and the archdeaconry. A diocese may be divided into three archdeaconries, twenty deaneries and four hundred parishes. The minister with oversight of the whole deanery is the rural dean and the clergy of the deanery meet in a deanery chapter.

This clergy chapter can sometimes be a forum for discussing ministry or theological issues, for social contact with people doing similar work in different places as well as a place for sharing resources, experience and information. Sadly some of them do not fulfil this function. They can be places where jealousies, rivalry and cynicism swamp any kind of mutual support. Those who feel they are not doing well or whose churches are struggling can be made to feel even more inadequate by the success stories of others, even if ostensibly told to give encouragement. Vicars are only human and most of them are still men. They are not very good at admitting pain or a sense of failure. But a clergy chapter which is characterised by honesty and sensitivity can be a support for its members.

With the changing and diverse forms of local ministry it is now sometimes unclear what the membership of the clergy chapter ought to be. Some chapters include retired clergy but in some places that would lead to the chapter being overrun by clergy no longer in parish ministry. Others will include non-stipendiary ministers. Bath and Wells diocese has a rural dean who does not receive a stipend. But then there are some parish clergy who work more closely with one or two of their Readers than they do with any other clergy in their parishes whose time is mostly given to their professional work. Then there is a question of whether these Readers should attend the chapter even if they cannot formally be members. Before it became a team ministry Wrockwardine deanery in Shropshire had a 'lesser chapter' of four clergy and a 'greater chapter' which included several Readers and the lay chair of the deanery synod. Chapters work out their own ways of dealing with the matter of membership and how they fix their meetings for the maximum benefit of the members.

Even with a clearly worked out role priority and a supportive ministry team or chapter it is still possible for country vicars to become so immersed in the work that they are unable to stand back and reflect on what is happening, or to feel swamped by the sheer volume of work that could be done. It is possible to be weighed down by unrealistic expectations even when one has discussed and agreed with others what the priorities are. It is possible to get depressed about the way that one is not achieving what one had hoped for within the parishes.

Working with a consultant can help clarify a vicar's thinking about the work. The consultant might be someone who specialises in this kind of work or they might be another vicar who takes on a mentor role. Some people operate what is called 'peer review', which is a meeting with a colleague to talk over the work. Co-consultancy is a slightly more structured variation on peer review. This is a situation in which two ministers meet and talk over their work, each helping the other see what they are doing from new angles, not telling each other what to do but trying to understand it from the other's perspective. By asking questions and trying to get a picture of what is happening and what the possibilities are, it is possible for one person to help another see the wood for the trees.

The intense nature of some personal work can affect a person's mind and emotions in ways that are hard to recover from without help. For this reason most people working in counselling or therapy have their own personal supervisor. This supervisor's task is not to make sure the person is working properly but to help them sort out what is happening to them. They are the counsellor's counsellor. Parish clergy, however, are not required to have pastoral supervisors and most do not, despite the fact that they have the additional pressure of living in the context in which they work, which many therapists and counsellors deliberately avoid. Another possible means of support for clergy is for them to have supervisors and, if these are not provided within a diocese, and they very rarely are, it is possible for clergy to find their own.

The wider church

The country vicar, together with the local church, is not just a part of a diocese but of a wider church: the Church of England, the whole Anglican Communion and the catholic Church which is the total community of all Christians. Even a diocese can be parochial in the common sense of the term and many clergy will find support, encouragement and vision from beyond it. Many clergy are helped by voluntary organisations and intentional communities as well as by conferences and common interest networks. These can provide opportunities to meet up with other people who are doing similar work and can help a vicar see things from different angles. They can have the particular strength of including not only clergy. The Rural Theology Association, for example, has a particular focus on ministry within the church in the countryside.[4] In such groups the country vicar can find others who know some of the particular pressures and difficulties of this kind of work, and this can be particularly helpful in a diocese which is largely geared up to addressing the needs of urban churches, or which assumes that the pattern of church life in the city or the suburbs is the norm. Other voluntary associations, catholic, evangelical, liberal or radical, can provide a context in which the vicar might feel theologically at home whilst also including the challenge and stimulus of including people who work in very different contexts. Intentional communities like the Franciscans, the Iona Community, the Benedictines and others have more of a family feel to them, with all the warmth and strain that that can involve, as well as a structure and a spiritual discipline. Books, journals and networks of correspondence by post or e-mail can all help vicars bring to their parishes both energy and insight from the wider church of which the local congregations are a part.

The Arthur Rank Centre in Warwickshire is an ecumenical organisation providing resources for rural churches.[5] The magazine *Country Way* which is produced by the Centre looks at the life of all churches in rural Britain, informing, encouraging and sparking off developments across denominations and in different parts of the country. Within their locality many country clergy will meet with and sometimes collaborate closely with the churches of other denominations. In many places the different churches work closely together, even sharing buildings as well as clergy and other ministers.

For much of its work local churches and their clergy can draw on the resources of other churches through publications, videos and the internet as well as meetings and conferences. Through these channels local churches can also contribute to the work of others in different places and a local church can be part of a network of local congregations encouraging each other, sparking ideas, sharing expertise and insight, and in many ways working together, even though they might never meet.

In his 1978 study of the church in the first century the New Testament scholar Gerd Theissen reckoned that there were two forms of church minister at that time, those who were local and those who moved from place to place.[6] The importance of this twofold structure was to ensure that the church was both rooted in a locality and had a connection with the wider movement. In an age when the only effective means of communication was through people actually travelling from place to place this was the only way it could be done. One of the weaknesses of the church in England through much of its history was that although the local church was legally and constitutionally a part of a wider organisation it was in many ways an independent unit: the parish church with its very settled parson. There was a local minister but no peripatetic ministers bringing news, insight and encouragement from other congregations. But in a society with good road networks, printing, television and computer links it is possible for the local church to be a part of the wider church life without wandering ministers moving from place to place. And it is possible for the country vicar to be both grounded in a local community and in touch with the wider life of the church, and to help other church members in this.

Apart from the vicar there are other ways in which local congregations can have links with other churches even across continents. Many rural congregations can tell of the stimulus to their own church life that came from a visit from someone from a very different place. Mission agencies work to enable people to exchange their skills and insights between churches, and organisations such as USPG and CMS can link local congregations with both individuals who have stories to tell and churches which are in very different social contexts. It is also likely to be the case that some members of a local congregation in rural England travel widely with their work or on holiday. And whilst many international travellers often see little of the country they are visiting other than the insides of hotels, cars and offices, they do sometimes gain a real insight into the life of the church in other places and these can be of help to local congregations, stimulating serious thought and questioning.

A place to live

Vicars who are not paid a full stipend but also work in other fields have an inevitable strong link with the secular world whatever their other occupation, but no clergy live and work solely within the church context. Any country vicar has a relationship with the wider secular world and a vicar living in a village will have to deal with rural life in much the same way that other people do. The bank, shops, library and garage will all probably be some distance away. There may be no local post office. All these affect the vicar's work, family and social life. There may be no pub or school nearby. A partner is likely to have to travel to work and there is unlikely to be a suitable bus service. Whilst the vicar lives in a big house and the diocese pays the council tax, the vicar is still having to manage on an income well below the national average in a place where costs are high. The vicar and the vicar's family are also having to build their social relationships within a small community where there may be few people with similar interests and some who are hard to get on with.

All this is the nature of rural life as people in the countryside experience it and the vicar shares that experience. It means that attempts to engage the Christian gospel with local issues are likely to come not simply from reflection and hearing what others have to say but also from the vicar's own experience. And whilst villages are all very different, and many people in rural areas live in isolated settlements and hamlets, a vicar in a village shares something of the delights and frustrations of small community life in the same part of the country as other parishioners.

There are sometimes suggestions that the clergy in rural areas should live in the towns and travel out to the village churches. This is often known as the minster model of church ministry as it is similar to that practised in minster churches in

the Middle Ages. It has the advantage for the clergy of providing them with a place to live where there are better facilities than in the villages and of having colleagues to work with.
However it has the disadvantage that the vicars of the country churches do not actually experience country life as their
parishioners do, and many people who move from the town
to the country are surprised by how significantly different that
is. With the minster model it is also possible for country
churches to have vicars who have never lived in the country
and only know what it is like at second hand. This does not
mean that they cannot therefore be effective ministers. Clergy
often have to deal pastorally with situations of which they
have no first-hand experience. But this fact does need to be
borne in mind in any church planning and reorganisation.

If the church did not provide housing for the clergy but
gave them instead a bigger stipend and left them to find their
own accommodation it would mean that in many areas of the
country the clergy would have to live in the towns or suburbs
because they could not afford to live in the countryside itself.
The vicars of country parishes would miss out on the experience of village life. However, it would give them first-hand
experience of another important aspect of many people's
lives: finding a home.

Nevertheless, while they are currently normally provided
with a house to live in, the clergy are not immune from
thought or anxiety about housing because at some point they
will retire and there might come a time when they need or
want to move out of parish ministry and then they will need
somewhere to live. Living in tied housing means that many of
them do not have a place in the housing market and being a
first-time buyer in middle age can be difficult. The Church
Commissioners currently have a scheme to assist the clergy
with housing in their retirement but it does not apply to
people who move out of parish ministry before that.

Colleagues outside the church

Until the nineteenth century country vicars had a crucial role
in the administration of welfare for the poor, in education and

often in providing rudimentary medical care. Now that work is taken over by government departments, local social services, education authorities and the health service, and country vicars will have some relationship with these bodies. The vicar might well be a school governor and also be involved in leading worship and other aspects of the education programme in a local school. In the pastoral support of individuals and families the vicar might be involved with social services or with the health service, with GPs or a hospital. In some situations the vicar might be treated as a local contact or a colleague by other service providers. Sometimes the vicar will be very much on the margins. To some extent this will depend on the attitude of the other practitioners but the vicar's own expertise, training and assumptions will also play a part.

It is crucial to any pastoral care that the carer is aware of his or her limitations. It is not helpful to anyone if a vicar assumes that simply by being ordained and appointed a vicar they have a particular expertise in pastoral work, community care or in teaching. They might not. Often it is important that the vicar leaves the medical practitioners, the social workers and the teachers to get on with the work for which they have been trained and in which they are experienced. Nevertheless the vicar might have an important contribution to make as a link with a family or local community, or as a priest, theologian or official church representative. And some clergy from their training and work before ordination or from subsequent study and experience do have a particular expertise they can offer. What is important is that clergy contribute what they can, respect the work of others and stay aware of their limitations. One of the values of the Herbert model of the country parson was that this minister had a holistic concern for people, valuing not just their souls but also their physical and mental well-being. The country vicar now can do the same but will do so together with other professionals.

Vicars can also learn a lot from people outside the church about aspects of their own work: teamwork and collaborative work-styles, managing people, administrative techniques, music, drama, teaching and counselling. With their particular concerns, interests and understanding of what they are doing clergy will adapt the techniques and skills others have developed and weigh up the approaches and ideas in the light of their theological understanding, but they cannot afford to ignore them any more than they can ignore the invention of the motor car, the telephone and the computer.

There are many ways they can tap into these insights, ranging from training courses run by associations and professional bodies, through courses run by local colleges or other educational agencies, to church-based training courses and literature of all kinds. Clergy will develop particular interests or find they have an aptitude for a particular kind of specialist work, or they may be aware of the need to be able to do more effectively and maybe efficiently what is an unavoidable part of their work. The resources are there. Sometimes diocesan training departments can point a vicar in the right direction. Sometimes it is colleagues or other members of the local church who will do this. Sometimes browsing bookshops or the internet or contact with local colleges can provide a way in. But as the key roles change for the local vicar as time goes on, so country vicars need to continually develop their insights and their skills.

The Sermon

There were no two ways about it – the bishop was good at this. The church was full and they were listening as he swept them across the global church. They heard of his recent visit to Kenya, of the scourge of AIDS and the liveliness of the churches. They were in the House of Lords where he was engaging with government about affairs of state. They were in a sixth-form college hearing with him the concerns and questions of young people and seeing how the Christian gospel related to them. This global church was alive and active.

Yes, numbers appeared to be down here in Britain but the press would say that, wouldn't they? The media cannot grapple with the subtleties. Sunday attendances were lower, but patterns were changing. More people came to midweek events. The congregation heard of office workers' services in the city centres, pram services in the suburbs, midweek communion for pensioners and family services on Saturday evenings.

Yes, the bishop did this well. The people were being encouraged. They were glimpsing an exciting world, very different from their normal weekly gatherings of twenty in their small country churches.

They were hearing now of the big gatherings. Spring Harvest, New Wine, Greenbelt, and the bishop's own Festival of the Word at the cathedral last year.

They were hearing a lot about the bishop, but this was an age of celebrities, and they were being presented here with their very own celebrity. They were hearing about some banter in a BBC studio and of how one vicar in the diocese had made it to the final in a panel game.

Maybe congregations needed this once in a while, but the

Archdeacon wasn't sure this was such an occasion. They were here because they had a new vicar. Stephen Watts was being inducted as vicar of their five parishes. He was there in the front row, with his wife and three children, and his parents were in the row behind. Such a nice young man. And what were the congregation expecting of him?

Probably much the same as Peter Soper and Chris Washman had done, only there had been two of them. Peter had had two parishes and Chris three. Stephen now had all five.

The congregation might now be expecting even more than Stephen's predecessors had given them, or at least hoping for something from this big and exciting Christian world they were glimpsing through the bishop's sermon. Midweek services. Young families. Innovations.

Maybe they weren't expecting anything like that. This was the country and maybe they thought exciting things like that didn't happen in country churches. Here they had to plod on, keeping the church going and supporting the vicar as best they could.

The bishop was coming to his conclusion. He was talking now about Stephen and his ministry in Leicester, and his family. He had the names right. Yes, this was an exciting time for any parish. It was an exciting time for the church.

This was what the congregation wanted to hear, though maybe it was not what it needed to hear. Maybe they needed to be told what it was realistic to expect of a vicar of five parishes. Maybe they needed to be told that behind the exciting events the bishop spoke of there was a lot of hard graft and prayer. Maybe they needed to be reminded that they, and not the bishop, were the church and that God was in this village as much as in Africa, the cathedral festival and the churches of suburbia.

But he was not the preacher. He was an archdeacon sitting and listening. The bishop was the preacher. And maybe the bishop had got it right.

The congregation certainly liked it.

169

10

Life and God

The fundamental question is: how might country vicars think about and understand their work in such a way that they can handle the pressures and remain constructive towards the church, their communities and themselves, balance their own needs with the demands and expectations of others, and retain their vision and passion for the gospel? I am suggesting that the country vicar's work is extensive and demanding but is often made harder by unrealistic expectations on the part of both parishioners and the vicar. These expectations stem from an inappropriate and out-of-date idea of what the vicar should be and do.

My suggestion is threefold. First, the vicar should be seen as a part of the church which is characterised by a community life, by worship and prayer and by learning in order to live with Christian faith. Second, within the local church the vicar can take on a dozen different roles to help the church carry out its task. Third, the vicar cannot take on all these roles and in a country area works within a number of local churches, so must decide which roles are the most important ones for the vicar in each parish at that particular time. The vicar will have regard for the views, needs and resources of the local churches, of the deanery and diocese, of the wider church, and of the wider society.

These four relationships are the frame in which the vicar works but they are not the only kinds of relationship in the vicar's life. Others are more fundamental to the vicar's well-being and the vicar's life and will have higher priority. One is the relationship of the vicar to what we might call the vicar's personal community. This will include family and close friends, many of whom do not live in the parishes and may not be members of the church. The second is the vicar's own self as a person with gifts, weaknesses, ideas, thoughts, emotions, a history and a future. The vicar brings these to the work but the person is much more than the work they do. The third relationship is with God. This has led to the person becoming a vicar in the first place, and might lead them out of it, but all other relationships exist within this one as God is the One who calls all things into being.

Personal community

Thinking about the hours that vicars work is difficult. It can be helpful occasionally for a vicar to audit how much time is being spent on different activities. Some might think themselves very busy with church work but when they analyse it they find that much of what they are doing is the kind of thing most other people do in their spare time. Some might feel they are bogged down by administrative work but when they tally up the hours find that in actual fact they are spending much more time in pastoral work or representing the church at various events in the parishes. The feeling that they are spending time in administration is more a reflection of the fact that they don't like it than it is of the hours spent at that kind of work.

But it is often difficult to decide what is to be classified as 'work'. Most vicars would probably think of prayer and church services as part of their work even though lay church members are expected to pray and go to church. But most vicars would probably not include repairing their car, although a farmer would certainly consider repairing a tractor as work and the vicar needs the car to get around the parishes. A vicar may not feel that reading theology books, journals or newspapers is really work, although a solicitor would most certainly consider keeping up to date on the law as an essential part of the job. Like many other people the vicar would probably consider working in the garden as a leisure activity, although in some villages if the vicar chose to let the vicarage garden run wild there would be serious grumbling about what was happening to 'God's acre'.

In order to have some clear space for themselves or their families many vicars tend to think in terms of working sessions: a session being a morning, afternoon or evening. The standard national working week is ten sessions, equivalent of a five-day week. In Britain today many people work more than that. Few vicars work that few. Vicars are required to have one day off every week and many will tend to be working for most of the other eighteen sessions. It has to be recognised that there are some vicars who do very little and it is possible for a vicar to get away with doing little more than taking Sunday services, weddings and funerals and attending four PCCs a year. But this is unusual. It is more likely that a vicar works about fifteen sessions, adding up to something like the average 56 hours discovered in the Rural Church Project:[1] the equivalent of a six-day week plus three evenings. This was the result of research carried out around 1990 among rural clergy and the work included preparing and leading services, pastoral work, administration, private prayer and study, community events, diocesan and deanery work and travel between activities.

Any discussion in a church about what the vicar might do needs to have within it a thought about how many hours or sessions in a week anyone should be expected to be working. It cannot be a precise science, partly because the boundaries between work and non-work are blurred but also because it is hard to make comparisons. The vicar does not have to travel to work, but at the same time the vicar cannot go home from work. The phone is always connected and even if there is an answering machine the vicar probably knows it is ringing and is wondering what the call is about. The office is joined on to the house and can be accessed at any time: the backlog of paperwork is not several miles away in another place. The vicar will go to social events within the parishes but will be known there as the vicar, even if not wearing the distinguishing clerical collar. The vicar might go with a friend or a partner but will still often be expected by parishioners to circulate and have a chat with them all, or at least be expected by some of them to hear the latest instalment of their ongoing personal crises. This can be hard on the partner as well as the vicar.

It is important that vicars are able to spend adequate time with members of their personal community. Children need time with their vicar mother or father. Partners need time when the vicar is not in role and not being shared with needy parishioners, so time off and holidays away are crucially important. Vicars must be able to maintain relationships with friends or family in other places, which can be difficult for someone who only has six weekends off a year including holiday periods. This can be hard when things are going well. If one is ill, if elderly parents are becoming frail, if a relationship is under strain, then more time must be given to this. Reasonable employers now have policies for compassionate leave. In the Church of England, while there might be diocesan policies with regard to maternity and paternity leave, in other situations the clergy have to decide for themselves what they do. In all situations they will have to make their own arrangements for cover or ask the rural dean to take over and usually they know the rural dean is also the vicar of another full group of parishes with their own demands.

One of the responsibilities of churchwardens is to make sure that the clergy have adequate pastoral care and support. Bishops in some dioceses cannot be contacted directly by their clergy outside office hours. Archdeacons and rural deans usually can. There are often diocesan counsellors who can be contacted by clergy in difficulty or for professional advice. But more important than these emergency services is the general well-being of the parish clergy and the opportunities they need for time out from church work, or the help they need to have a life which includes church work within it. Churchwardens and other church leaders can help the parish clergy in this, not least by challenging unrealistic expectations by other people. This is hard to do if the vicar will not discuss his or her work with the churchwardens.

Relationships with one's personal community are not just a

matter of time. There are other pressures on these relationships as a result of the vicar's work and role within a community. Children can be subject to bullying or ostracism by other children because their mother or father is a vicar, or subject to unhelpful expectations on the part of adults. It can still be assumed in some rural communities that a vicar's wife will fit into a particular niche or role. This is less likely of a vicar's husband as that is a relative novelty and the stereotypes do not exist. The mere fact that vicars often have to go away from their parishes in order to have a holiday can create difficulties, both because of cost and the fact that a few days off at home is not a possibility. Some vicars feel they cannot go home but can only sometimes get away.

It will sometimes happen that much that the vicar would like to do and many of the things that other church members would like the vicar to do simply are not possible because the vicar's personal community needs to have first call on the person's time and energy. This person is doing the work of a vicar within a wider framework of personal relationships with friends and family. The friends and family are not an add-on extra to the vicar's work life, although it can sometimes feel like that to a vicar and the vicar's personal community.

Taking on roles

Without analysing the various possibilities many vicars are aware that they take on different roles within their churches and that they are more comfortable with some than others. They feel that they wear different hats on different occasions, some of which they like and others they don't, and sometimes they are confused about which one they are being expected to wear. There are times when they feel like asking someone in a conversation which hat they want them to wear. Does this person want them to be the Chair of School Governors, a pastor or simply a friendly neighbour, a source of information on church history and practice or someone who will help them talk through their present frustration? Moving from one role to another and giving priority of time and energy to some rather than others is something that many people, including vicars, do instinctively.

The vicar is not playing a part, pretending to be something other than they are. We are talking here about role in the way that a group of people in a meeting might take different roles with different responsibilities. One takes the chair and tries to make sure the meeting addresses the issues on the agenda, that all are able to contribute their part, that the group moves forward in its thinking and that decisions are made and action will follow. The secretary meanwhile needs to make sure that a record is kept, that previous decisions are kept to or deliberately revised, and ensures that the guiding rules are adhered to. The treasurer has a watching brief on the financial implications of possible courses of action and of decisions. Then within the group other people may take on different informal roles. One is the ideas person, often able to outline several different ways in which something could be done, thinking laterally and imaginatively. Another might be good at seeing why something will not work. Others will be aware of how other people beyond the group might feel about a decision. Others are good at making sure that tasks are finished.

All this is well worked out in management theory and in the practice of organisations from IBM to village hall committees. Within a local church the vicar takes on a number of similar roles, both in the church's meetings and in its whole life. In a sports team some players are all-rounders, others are specialists. But even the specialists could play in other positions if necessary. Someone who plays three-quarter in a local league rugby team could well play in the pack if their local pub is turning out a team for a friendly against a team from over the hill. In a team people are ideally playing to their strengths but if there are gaps or weaknesses people will play other positions. Even in a strong team a player may move out of role in an extreme situation. No one is going to neglect the chance to score simply because their role is principally to provide the ball to other players. Whilst a vicar will have particular strengths, he or she will at times need to take on less preferred roles.

Switching between roles involves a person bringing different aspects of their personality to the fore. Everyone's personality can be thought of as made up of a number of sub-characters. Some of these are obvious and often seen. Others are hidden away and only emerge occasionally. People who behave one way at work can seem to become someone different at a sports match, or at home, or in a crisis. They have not become someone else, but aspects of their personality appear which are normally hidden. The person may be aware of this and sometimes a person can have other aspects of their personality move centre stage in a way that disturbs them moments or hours later. They did not realise they could be like that. But reflecting on this afterwards can lead them to better self-understanding.

Some people find studies like the Myers Briggs Typology Indicator or the Enneagram help them become more aware of the aspects of their character which are hidden and those which are apparent, and also how these relate to each other. It can also help them understand why other people behave the way they do. Some psychological theories, like psychosynthesis and analytical psychology, involve a conception of the person as a cluster of sub-personalities, some of which are often visible to others and some of which are hidden. These theories seek to explain not only how personalities are made up but also why it is that different people find different activities demanding or energising. But even without a knowledge of these theories many people are aware that they come across differently at work from how they do at home, or with their in-laws, or in a church meeting. Every person can be thought of as like a small group of characters, each one coming to the fore in different kinds of circumstances.

This kind of self-understanding can help an individual vicar or others with whom the vicar works decide which roles and what kind of work would suit them best. Like the team members playing to their strengths it makes sense, as far as possible, for a group of ministers to work at the kind of tasks to which they are most suited. Most people are aware that among the many things they do they find some tiring, others exhilarating, others stressful and others relaxing. And they also know that other people are different in this respect.

According to the theories derived from Jungian psychology a fundamental difference between people is that between the introvert and the extravert. The introvert finds face-to-face dealing with people tiring, the extravert finds it energising. The tired introvert wants to stay in and watch the television or read a book. The tired extravert wants to go to a party. The introvert likes to think and then talk. The extravert finds it hard to think without talking.

Vicars are in the position of often being able to balance how they do their work. They will have days which are wall-to-wall encounters with other people and other days when they are at a desk working through paper, quietly preparing for future services or planning a particular project. But most days can be a mixture of different activities. They are sometimes able to balance out those things which they find energise them with the things they find tire them, and they can try to have space for a pick-up after something which might be seriously depressing. It is also sometimes possible for vicars to choose to do those things which they find the most interesting and exciting and reduce to the minimum those they find demanding or tedious. If they do this they are likely to be able to work longer hours and retain a sense of humour and enthusiasm than if they are mostly doing work they find emotionally draining.

However, this might not be the best thing for the local church and the local community. The vicar who loves arranging rotas and redesigning services on the computer could keep at it for hours but there might be other things about their parishes which need doing. Other vicars might choose to be out and about as much as possible because this is what gives them a buzz and they know that people appreciate it, but if the organisation of the church is in disarray and badly prepared sermons are tedious and uninspiring they might not actually be doing the best thing for their parishes. It makes sense for vicars to be able to play to their strengths as much as possible but they are not there simply to amuse themselves, nor are they the only players. There are others in the local church who also need to be able to develop and use their gifts and that might mean the vicar making space for them, whether it be in leading worship, pastoral visiting, administration or engaging in local politics. There are also things which will need doing and which the vicar might not find enjoyable or easy but which no one else is in a position to do.

Vicars have their own preferred way of working and their own gifts. In working out what roles in a parish a vicar should take the vicar and the church are foolish if they do not make use of the vicar's particular gifts, be they in worship, teaching, in community work or resourcing the church for its work. Anyone considering the vicar's work also needs to have in mind that different people prefer to operate in different ways. Some people love routine and quickly become exhausted if they cannot live by a pattern. Others become quickly bored with routines, preferring to be continually responding to immediate demands or developing new ways of doing familiar tasks. Some want a clear framework in which to work and to know what is expected of them. Others want a general direction to move in and to be able to work out their own way of going there. Some want to be always doing things with other people or continually telling others what they are up to. Others prefer to be left alone to get on with things and find it much harder if they have to work with other people. An understanding of different kinds of personality is helpful here. That may come from a well-developed system of personality profiling but there is also a degree of common sense and folk wisdom about recognising that people are all different, that it's a matter of horses for courses and of not trying to round up sheep with a terrier.

In working out the importance of the different roles within a church often a compromise needs to be reached. A vicar might have a strong sense that one or two particular roles are important, perhaps because of how they understand the nature of the church or because of how they see the local church's needs. These views may differ from those of other members of the local church. In such cases vicars will not disregard their own understanding but will also need to respect the views of others and work out a balance between the two.

Styles of ministry and the vicar's theology

When put together, some of the various roles of the country vicar form a particular style of ministry. A vicar who takes on the roles of a manager, administrator and leader might well be seen as a kind of general secretary of the local churches. Another vicar who is more concerned with teaching and training local congregations so that the basic pastoral ministry and regular worship of the church can go on independently of the local vicar could be seen to be focusing more on building up the church. Another might come to see their role much more in terms of being available to people as a community chaplain and as an informal teacher, and therefore as a friendly neighbourhood theologian. Another might see their ministry as being a kind of spiritual guide, perhaps a counsellor-cum-theologian. Another, with a concern for their own style of life, their family and home life, and believing it important to be able to stop and chat or potter about the village, might see their life not in terms of what they do but as what they are, and see the ordained ministry as a matter of being rather than doing. In leading worship some clergy draw on the resources of the Iona Community which arise partly from a concern which the founder George MacLeod expressed as 'finding new ways to touch the hearts of all', and also from a passion for justice and peace and a respect for the integrity and value of creation. Many of the people who compose these prayers, songs and meditations are also very active in campaigning for social change.

In his study of George Herbert, *The Country Parson*, Anthony Russell[2] argued that the country vicar today needs to take on four roles advocated by Herbert, that of priest, pastor, teacher and shepherd or leader. This was a distillation of Herbert's parson for the twentieth century, discarding much that Herbert attempted as being unnecessary and drawing out from Herbert's manifesto the features that Russell considered particularly pertinent for the time. Some country vicars will go along with this.

Many vicars have approaches to their work which they have developed over a long time. These derive from an interplay of their own preferences with their theological understanding of the church and the ordained ministry. Clergy have their own views of what the church is about and what they were ordained to be and to do. Some will rarely articulate them. Others will be quite explicit that they hold to a catholic view of the church and its sacraments, or that they see the essence of the church in its evangelical commission to preach the gospel to all nations, or that they see the church as a servant of society and themselves as servants of the church. There are various possibilities.

According to Avery Dulles the church can be seen as an institution, a mystical communion, a sacrament, a herald, a servant, and the vanguard of the kingdom of God.[3] Most clergy would probably agree to all of these, but have their own priorities. For some it is the mystical communion that is its fundamental character, the church in its prime form being in the interaction of people with each other and with God. For others the church's sacramental character is its essence, while for still others the church fundamentally exists to proclaim the gospel. Some might want to add to Dulles' list, maybe seeing the church principally as a community of spiritual pilgrims or a community of disciples.

A different emphasis will give a different slant to a vicar's work and different basic priorities, but if the church is all these things they can expect that at some time in some places they will need to take on roles which are not the most obvious ones according to their own theological inclination but are the most necessary in that time and place. The sacramentalist might need to be principally an evangelist in one parish at one time. The vicar who would prefer to speak about God might need to help the church stop talking and get on with a piece of practical work for the local community. A vicar whose concern is that the church serve its community might find that time needs to be spent organising and administering the institution so that it can effectively do this. This is not to say that vicars have to go against the grain of their theological understanding but that they need to recognise that this is a matter of emphasis, and that sometimes they have to give priority to what they see as generally a less significant aspect of the church's life.

It is also quite possible that a person espouses a view of the church and can explain why, in theological terms, the church should be seen in that way but is actually drawn to that view because it suits their personality. This is not to suggest they do it deliberately but the development of ideological studies has alerted us in recent decades to the way that people often proclaim views and base their actions on what is to their advantage, whilst believing that they are being impartial. This happens in politics and international diplomacy and it happens in the church.

So it is possible that a vicar who believes fervently that an ordained minister is someone set apart with a sacred function also needs this difference from others to strengthen their sense of personal identity. It is possible that a person with a firm view that the church is entrusted with timeless truths is also afraid of uncertainty. It is possible that someone who sees their ordained ministry as essentially supportive of a local church working quietly within its wider community is fearful of having to stand out from the crowd, of hostility or of criticism.

People have their different gifts, their strengths and their weaknesses. No one is a totally rounded, omnicompetent human being. The ordained ministry does not require people to be other than they are. The point is simply that ordained ministers have their own gifts, their weaknesses, their preferences and their areas of vulnerability, some of which they may recognise and some they may not. They also have a vested interest in their views of the church and its life because these have been developed through long study and experience and they might also suit them as a person. It will clearly help the clergy and their churches if they continue to develop their theology and also come to know themselves better.

Gifts and strengths

Some people are very clear in their mind about what they can do well and what they struggle with. Some are not at all clear. There are clergy who believe they cannot preach, perhaps because they are not like a minister who inspired them greatly when they were a student, but when they are forgetting about their style and their method and are simply speaking honestly with other people they are excellent communicators. There are others who feel that they do not get on with other people easily when in fact the discomfort they feel in groups stems from deeply buried experiences of their early years, and other people actually love to have them around. There are those who think they are not good organisers because they are always aware of the things that go wrong, whereas everyone else feels very comfortable with what is happening and is clear about their own part in it. There are ministers who do not believe that they are good evangelists because the certainties that they once held have now left them, but their struggling conversations about God are both enlightening and encouraging for their parishioners, who feel this is a person who is simply one step ahead of them on the journey rather than someone who has already arrived at where they will never be.

Like anyone else clergy need help to realise what their gifts are. In many situations they get little of this. People sit politely during sermons, indicating little by their body language, and simply saying 'Thank you' or 'Nice sermon' at the end of the service. Liturgies, administrative work, telephone conversations, funerals, business meetings – all these pass, completed, often with little feedback and the vicar having little idea of what is being done well and how things could be improved. In some places people are better at giving this kind of helpful response than in others. In some churches a few members of a congregation might want to discuss with the vicar what has been said in a sermon, or the churchwardens might feel confident enough to tell the vicar how things are going, saying what is going well as well as what is going badly. But there are vicars who only realise how much their ministry is appreciated and how helpful it has been when they announce that they are leaving for another job. Others only hear criticism or hear nothing at all. This might be because parishioners feel the vicar is up on a pedestal and they would no more criticise or compliment the vicar to his face than they would the doctor. It may be because the people of that area rarely say anything to each other about whether they have done something well or badly, but just take things as they come and do not think to judge.

Those who do have a sense of their own strengths and weaknesses can say to themselves or to their church members 'I can do that,' or 'I think it would be better if someone else did it.' Some vicars are aware that they have a particular flair for some aspect of the church's work and a church is foolish if it does not give the vicar opportunities to develop it. But vicars are often in situations where a whole multitude of things need to be done and they are the only one who is likely to do them. Their particular gifts might then be neglected or only emerge on rare occasions. That can be frustrating, but vicars are not the only ones who have to live with that kind of frustration and many of their parishioners probably feel the same way.

God

Vicars will think about their work, about the local church and about their possible roles in the light of what they believe about God, the world and the church. But there are times when it is not a matter of thinking about God but of facing God. This might happen in a crisis. It might happen under pressure or stress or in a state of great joy. It might be in worship or out in the parish. It might be in the vicar's regular prayers.

It would have been in response to God that the person became a vicar in the first place. There will be times during a person's ministry when they will seriously question this. They will bring to God the question of whether they ought to be doing this kind of work at all, or whether they can. And amidst the possibilities for them in their particular location they will lay the dilemmas before God and look for wisdom or vision as to what they should do. And in the end, when the vicar has talked about the work with leaders of the local church and has thought through the possibilities in the light of his or her own understanding of what is happening in the parishes, in the wider church and the world, the vicar will make a decision.

Sometimes these decisions are quick. There is no great anxiety or weighing up of possibilities. Day by day, hour by hour, decisions are made and patterns develop. But sometimes the vicar will need to stand back and assess what has been happening up until then and try to see which way they should go next. Jesus withdrew to the desert after his baptism and at other crucial moments in his ministry. For parish clergy there are plenty of places where they can go on retreat and many vicars will have their favourites. Retreats can be for recharging personal energy and for reflection and decision-making about the shape of their ministry. Many clergy have spiritual directors whom they visit regularly to help them focus on their relationship with God.

This relationship with God is not in addition to the others in which the vicar works. God is present in all the others. The vicar operates within a number of circles: the parishes, the diocese, the wider church and the secular world, and God encircles these. The vicar lives in relationship not only to the church but to friends, family and neighbours, as well as to the vicar's own history and future possibilities, and God encompasses all these. So at times the vicar looks beyond them to God who is their ground and the creator of all, who is known in Jesus Christ and who is continually at work within and beyond all relationships by the Spirit.

The principal characteristic of God is love. Any relationship with God is founded not on achievement but on grace. In the end, when vicars have worked out what their principal roles are to be in particular situations they have to translate this into a way of working. A multitude of daily decisions have to be made about what to do and what to leave. It is possible for a vicar, like anyone else, to fall into the error of thinking that a feeling of guilt is an indicator of a sin or failing. A vicar might feel guilty about not visiting someone during their illness. This is perhaps deep in their mind as one of the essential things that vicars do, though in actual fact it might be that the person would not have wanted a visit and might have been embarrassed by it. Or the person might have welcomed it but the training of lay pastoral visitors, finding a new churchwarden, or organising a good Christingle for the children was actually more important. Or a vicar may feel continually uneasy about the backlog of unanswered mail lying on their desk, even though the stuff they have postponed is not at all urgent, or even needing any attention at all. Deciding priorities and using them as a guide is likely to involve living with unease or even feelings of guilt.

One way of approaching this is to hit it head on and decide what is not going to be done. The Companions of Brother Lawrence have a concept of 'planned neglect'.

> In order to live a fully rounded life, life as God intends it to be, we must include things other than our work. This almost inevitably means leaving something undone. For us, planned neglect will mean deliberately choosing which things we will leave undone or postpone, so that instead of being oppressed by a clutter of unfinished jobs, we think out our priorities under God and then accept without guilt or resentment the fact that much that we had thought we ought to do we must leave.
>
> We shall often be tempted into guilty feelings when we take time off. But we should then remind ourselves that such guilt is a sin against the generosity of the Spirit, and also extremely infectious.[4]

And those clergy who feel themselves to be in a parental role towards their parishioners would do well to remind themselves that the understanding now is not that people need 'excellent' but 'good enough' parents.[5] One educational psychologist has said that she brought up her children on the basis of benign neglect.[6] Children need to develop a certain toughness and self-sufficiency, and so do churches. Parish clergy who are trying to do too much are helping neither their churches nor themselves.

Hours

Angela Watson had decided she needed to talk this out. She had been the Vicar of Pusham for three years now and lived in the parish.

She was also Vicar of Fixley, where a small group of people maintained the building, ran a choir, visited newcomers and met on Sundays for worship.

And of Upton Parva, with a population of 107 at the last count, half of whom were cousins, and who always seemed surprised to see her.

She was Vicar of Limpley Green, where a dedicated band of church members continually tried to involve the other residents of the parish in village life and were continually disappointed but still came to church, contributed generously to maintain the building and pay their parish share, and prayed for revival.

And of Broxton, where the school and the shop had closed, the pub had become an expensive restaurant, and only the parish church remained as a public building. There the church members organised four events a year for all the parish, ranging from beetle drives to pie suppers and the occasional concert. Angela was amazed to see how it was possible to serve pie and chips and play beetle in a church full of pews.

Then there was Pusham.

When the storms came in November the churchwarden of Fixley rang her up on the Saturday to tell her not to worry when she saw the gap in the roof. A man was coming on Monday to fix it. In Pusham the churchwarden rang her the next morning to tell her there were some tiles lying in the churchyard.

The time had come to talk about this with the PCC, so Angela made a list of all the different kinds of things she seemed to be expected to do. It was a long list, and there were three columns for PCC members to tick. One was for things that Angela did not need to do because other people could. One was for things that Angela had to do. And the other was marked desirable but not essential.

She gave these to the PCC and asked them to spend a few minutes ticking the columns and then she collated the results. Some of them did not think it was essential for her to get out the cups for coffee after the midweek communion. And there was a consensus view that someone else could set mousetraps. Otherwise nearly everyone seemed to think that she ought to do almost everything on the list.

So she asked the next question she had lined up. How many hours a week did they think she ought to work?

There was a silence, and a lot of puzzled expressions. It looked as if no one had thought about this before. Ever. She hadn't said they should bear in mind that she had two teenage children and a husband who worked in Coventry. She wanted no concessions. Just a fair answer.

Bill Yateman finally answered.

'Eighty-four,' he said.

There was nodding among many of the PCC members. Not because this seemed like a right answer but because Bill Yateman had spoken and was a respected and longstanding PCC secretary who had once been an agricultural adviser, and he knew about these things.

Angela waited, and after a few seconds there was an explosion from the corner of the room. Robert had come recently to the village having joined a dental practice in Dorminster.

'You can't expect anyone to work eighty-four hours a week!' he said.

'People aren't going to stop dying because the vicar wants time off.' said Bill. 'God doesn't take time off.'

This was theology and Angela was on home ground now.

'He does in the Bible,' she said. 'He rests on the seventh day of creation and demands that his people keep the Sabbath. And any- way, I'm not God.'

11

Work, Vocation and Justice

Work and vocation

The vicar comes to the work of ministry as a person within a network of relationships with family and friends, as an individual with particular gifts and insights, and in a relationship with God. This network will change over time and people themselves change, but these relationships predate the person becoming a vicar. The person's life is bigger than their work as a vicar and it needs to stay that way. Being a vicar is a job that some priests do.

For some people any talk about the vicar having a job seems to devalue the work, as if someone were saying it is 'just a job'. The musician who gets a job with a good orchestra, a surgeon who has a job at a teaching hospital or a lawyer who is promoted to lead the legal team of a large insurance company would not say these are 'just a job', and neither will a priest about an appointment as a college or hospital chaplain or as the vicar of five parishes.

For others it might seem like a threat to the idea of vocation. It is often said that being a vicar is not a job – it is a vocation. Vicars, it is said, cannot really be 'off duty'. At any time they might get involved in a pastoral or theological conversation, or an emergency might arise. If vicars thought about their work as a job where would they draw the boundaries? What about prayer and Bible study, caring for their neighbours and worshipping God in church services? All these things are expected of lay church members as well, who are also supposed to be able to give an account of their own faith should the need or opportunity arise.

Many other church members can also become 'on duty' at any moment and others live on the job. Farmers have to deal with problems with livestock at any time and any conversations in the local community might relate to their work, their land or their business. But that does not mean one cannot talk about the farmer's work, or the job of being a farmer. It certainly is more a way of life than many other occupations which involve attending a particular place, doing set tasks and then coming home at the end of the day or the shift. But no farmer thinks in terms of working all the time. The skittles match and the family party, the shoot or the hunt are not 'work', they are leisure. A blurred boundary between work and leisure is a feature of life for many other people in small communities as well, but they are still able to think in terms of having time off and of times of work.

Behind this fear of talking about the vicar's work sometimes lie two unhealthy tendencies which are encouraged by the way that the word 'lay' has now come to refer to the members of the church who are not clergy. The word originally meant all the church members, including those who were ordained. The Greek *laos* was the whole people of God. Having a mindset in which the church consists of lay people and clergy as two separate kinds of Christian can encourage church members who are ordained and those who are not to think of their lives in different ways. The clergy, because they are always at the front during worship and have the authority to preside at the sacraments and to preach, can easily slip into thinking that they are somehow more important. They do not have something as mundane as a job – they have a vocation, and the deference with which some other church members treat them does nothing to reduce this sense of pride. And those who are not ordained can avoid taking their own Christian discipleship seriously if they think it is only a special group of people which has a vocation.

If we are to talk about vocation we can do so in three ways. The first is the vocation of every person to become what they

190

potentially can be, developing the gifts given them by God the Creator, and rising to the challenges and opportunities of their particular situation in life.

There is also the vocation to a particular role or occupation within society and within the church. It is clearly the case that many teachers, medical workers, social workers and artists have just as strong a sense of vocation as do many clergy. They are clear this is what the Creator wants them to be doing. In its recent strategy document on education the General Synod has called on the church as a whole to encourage people to explore whether they might have a vocation to become a teacher.[1]

In the ordination service candidates are asked if they believe they are called by God to the ordained ministry. This same question is asked of those who go on to be vicars as of the many clergy who become hospital, school, university or forces chaplains, who teach in colleges or work for mission agencies, who combine their ordained ministry with paid employment in some other field or who live off their pension or investments. The vocation to being ordained is a broad sense of calling. It is not necessarily about being a vicar.

But someone might have a sense that a particular job is God's work for them at the present time. For clergy that might mean becoming or remaining the vicar of a certain group of parishes. Thinking about what kinds of work that might involve, and weighing up the relative importance of the different roles which the vicar might take within the parishes, is a way of taking very seriously that aspect of vocation.

Prayer

It is in relationship to God that people discover and develop their vocations. Some people have significant insights during prayer or worship. Others find themselves being steered in a certain direction by the suggestions of other people or their own sense of what they can do and what they enjoy doing, in a deep sense and not simply in a shortlived thrill. For others it comes from an awareness of what is needed in the church or the world and a sense that they have a part to play in God's meeting of that need. Some people see an advert for a job and think that might be the thing for them and accept it as such when others make the decision to appoint them. But however this sense of vocation comes, prayer, the deliberate attending to God in thought, imagination or words, will have a part.

It will also have a part in the working out of the vocation day by day. Prayer can be seen as the regular attending to the music of God which is the background to life or aligning oneself with the direction of the Spirit of God. There are many ways of praying. Much is written on the subject and there is no shortage of retreats, courses and conferences for clergy who want help in developing their prayer life. According to the rule of St Benedict prayer is work, but whether or not prayer is properly seen as part of the vicar's job is a question which would only need an answer if vicars somehow worked to set hours. While vicars need to ensure that they are not consumed by their work but that their work is a part of their lives, they are never going to have clear boundaries of what is counted as work or as leisure. Vicars will spend time in prayer both for their parishes and for themselves and many will probably count prayer as crossing the boundaries.

It might be that the local church leadership, whether they are a PCC or a group of churchwardens, place little store by prayer and worship, or by study. They might see themselves as simply maintaining an institution for the benefit of the parish, or even for their own benefit, but this is unlikely. There must be something about the church's worship and about what the church has been in the past and could be in the present which draws people to be involved and encourages them to take the kind of responsibilities that churchwardens and others take. If it is only ancient monuments they are interested in, then there are probably old castles, houses and megaliths about the area for them to expend their energies on.

Prayer, study and worship for the vicar were important aspects of the life of Herbert's country parson and are likely to be seen as such by many church members today, even if they do not often pray themselves or read much. A discussion of what is and is not possible for the local vicar is actually likely to release the vicar to spend time in prayer and study. Without such discussion a vicar might not leave reflective space for study and prayer, or when they do give these time they might feel they are doing it despite the wishes of their parishioners. And if in discussion the local church leaders do say they think this is wasted time then it opens the door for a fascinating exploration of what the church is actually about, of what is meant by prayer, and how we might develop our understanding of what it means to be Christian.

There is also the possibility that lay church members will point out to their vicar that they pray, and they do a full day's work. This is a fair comment that some clergy need to hear. On average country clergy work hours far in excess of the recommended maximum for good health and beyond the European legal limit, but so do a lot of other people in the countryside, including many farmers and others running their own businesses. Getting this view out into the open can give rise to useful discussion about the pressures of work and what it is reasonable to expect of another person. If vicars place a great deal of importance on their own healthy lifestyle, on their family and home life, and maybe maintaining their garden or other personal interest, then let them defend this in an open discussion rather than simply allow unspoken resentment to develop. If this is an important part of their Christian discipleship and their being an ordained minister then they should be able to explain why, and use this as an opportunity to help other people assess their own way of life.

Many people are not as free to adjust their lifestyle as some clergy are. They are on a treadmill of work to try to earn the money to pay their bills or their debts. An open discussion of this can perhaps open to them other possibilities, like changing occupation. Or it might help them realise that while they resent the hours they have to work they are still doing it with a certain degree of choice. Or if they are cornered and have no choice but to keep working excessive hours then maybe the minds of others in the discussion can be opened to how life is for some in their community. This might affect their attitude, their own willingness to work within the community or the church, and maybe even how they vote. In such a discussion, which may well become an emotional exchange, work might be done to try to root Christian faith in the lives of the people in that particular community. Or it might simply be a time for the vicar and others to listen and hear how life is for some of their fellow church members. Not a time for answers, or even sympathy, but a time for compassionate solidarity, marked by respectful silence.

Authority

As an ordained minister a vicar is subject to the authority of the bishop. In the phraseology of the ordination service, the clergy's oaths of allegiance and the licensing service there is still an echo of feudalism.[2] In a feudal society everyone had to belong to someone else and the priest was the bishop's man. So there is talk in the church about 'canonical obedience' to the bishop and some clergy would see themselves as something akin to the bishop's representative, required to obey the bishop's instructions in all church matters. They might find rather weak the idea that vicars should work out their parish ministry with regard to diocesan policy rather than in obedience to the bishop.

However, there is also within the Church of England a strong strand of independence on the part of the parish clergy. The vicar's freehold was a defence against authoritarian bishops, and one of the reasons that many clergy are reluctant to see the freehold removed without some other protection in its place is that they want to retain that degree of independence. In the nineteenth century there were court cases over the introduction of various Catholic rites and ceremonies into the Church of England. In these it was often those clergy who would hold to a high doctrine of episcopal authority who were disobeying their bishop and introducing vestments or candles where they had not been before. During the twentieth century many clergy were pleased to have the protection of the civil law in being able to marry people who had been divorced when their bishop did not support it. They could do so knowing that the bishop could not penalise them. The church also has a history of clergy with radical or social-ist politics arguing their views and campaigning in dioceses headed by Tory bishops and ignoring the bishop's instruction that they desist from such activities. So while there still remains an idea of the clergy belonging to the bishop and being required to obey the bishop in all things lawful and honest, in practice for a long time the parish clergy have oper-ated with a high degree of independence. Because of this many bishops would be reluctant to demand that any of their clergy obey them in a particular matter that was not one of significant principle.

What is now needed is for the rules and rites to catch up with the reality of the situation. Whilst archaic legal practices and rituals might be quaintly entertaining or reassuring for those who want to see the church as a link with a mythical past, they often do not provide the framework which is nec-essary for the care and protection of the clergy and for the effective working of the clergy within a diocese. The current reworking of the terms and conditions of work of the parish clergy needs to be based not on a feudal concept of belonging to the bishop but on proper employment legislation. These changes should enable the clergy of the Church of England to have the security of employment which other workers enjoy and also enable dioceses to develop strategies for the deploy-ment of clergy which balance the needs of the diocese as a whole with those of individual parishes and the clergy. Within that relationship and with proper capability proce-dures in place, it should be possible for the parish clergy to develop their ways of working with regard to both their local situations and the needs of the diocese and for the diocesan management to ensure that the clergy are working effectively.

Justice
It is a long road from being a 'lay' church member to be-coming a vicar. There are now various routes a person might

follow to become one. The journey will normally have involved a thorough selection process and several years of study. Once ordained the person will normally then have spent three years or more working as a curate under the direction and supervision of an experienced vicar. Curates and vicars have given over their gifts, time and often their careers to work in this way for the church. Their families have also paid a high price.

The church has also invested a lot in them, though not as much as many organisations spend in the training of their employees. Clergy in training do not receive a stipend until they are ordained. If they had undertaken their theological studies full-time they would have managed solely on grants, and many people training for ordination experience serious financial hardship. Even though most clergy are paid less than they would have earned if they had stayed in their previous employment or had spent the same amount of time training for another occupation, they are still not cheap. In most organisations the salaries of the workforce are the biggest expense and this is true of the Church of England. In every diocese clergy stipends and housing are three-quarters of the budget. Clergy pensions account for a large part of the rest. The remainder is support and administration. In most parishes the local church's contribution towards that is by far the biggest part of its budget, only to be overtaken occasionally when there is a major building project going on.

Part of the church's mandate is to seek and develop justice. The theme runs through the Bible from the Books of the Law to Revelation. Unfortunately it is often hidden by the tendency to translate the Hebrew word *sedeq* and the Greek word *dikaiosune* as 'righteousness', with its association of individual moral purity, rather than as 'justice' with its association with community building and action. The justice of which it speaks is not a nice balance of equal shares but an attitude and actions which stem from God's concern for those who suffer. The church has a chequered history but it can look to many occasions when it has been a great force for this kind of justice, from the early church's support of widows and orphans through to the campaigns against slavery and the exploitation of children. At various times in national debates the Church of England tries to make a contribution based on a sense of God's compassionate justice. Few would suggest that it does not at the same time need to look for this justice in its own life.

This works out at both parish and national level. The local church needs to have concerns beyond its own life. A church which is only concerned with its own survival is as good as dead already. God's concern is for the world and the church needs to share that concern and its members need to act accordingly. In many country parishes this happens as church members involve themselves in local government, in supporting and working for charities, in schools, homes and hostels, and in national political campaigning. And like the church at national level the local church needs to organise itself and act in ways which are just and fair.

The church is not acting with justice if the clergy have to live the whole time with the feeling that other people expect more of them than they can possibly do. It is simply a matter of justice that what is expected of them is within their capabilities. It is only fair that they have adequate support for their work, both from other church members and from their diocese. They ought to be able to have the same expectation of reasonable pay and working conditions as their parishioners.

All vicars have a lot they can contribute to the life of the local church. A vicar comes to a parish with a range of gifts and insights. It only makes sense for the local church to work with the vicar, for whom they are paying through their parish share, so that the vicar can work most effectively with them. And it is both justice and sense for the rural clergy to work as well as they can at their part in the church's mission.

At the local level this means vicars together with other church members clarifying priorities and getting on with the jobs that need to be done, developing their theological understanding and their skills and through prayer, reflection and study continuing their own spiritual journeys. Parishioners not only need technically skilled practitioners but also ministers who recognise and are exploring the life of God. Only people on their own spiritual journeys can help others on theirs. Vicars need to have adequate time and space for this exploration whilst making their unique contribution to the work of the local church.

How effectively the country clergy are able to work with their local congregations, how well they can work out what contribution they can best make to the church's mission in that place, and how they can develop their own skills, their thinking and their spiritual lives depends not only on the vicars themselves. Vicars have a key part to play but it is not just up to them. How well the local vicar can play his or her part depends also on how willing the local church is to work with its clergy and how well the clergy are supported by the diocese.

The rural church has always been changing but that change has been particularly rapid in the last forty years. Change will continue. How the church in rural England will develop in the next forty years is not known. But however it changes it will need clergy who will join in the life of the local church, work with the other members in carrying out its mission in that locality and link it with the life of the wider church. In doing this they will take on different roles according to the needs and opportunities in different places and at different times. They will be involved in the community life of the area and of the local churches, in the church's worship and prayer, and have a part to play in helping church members discover what it means for them to be disciples of Jesus in their place and time. The vicar's task is not to be the church but to help the church live out its Christian faith.

Ministry Review

Peter Fynn was sitting in the Archdeacon's study and they were talking over the two years since his induction.

Peter's first year had gone very well. People were friendly. A few had called round with cards and Helen was given a pot plant and two bunches of flowers. The following Sunday there were a lot of people at church. The number declined slowly over the next few months but there were now one or two people in the churches who, it seemed, had not been to church for some time before. They were younger than most of the congregation and there were two young couples who talked very keenly about having a Sunday school.

Helen had managed to bring their children to church most weeks and the youngest explored under the pews and piled up the hassocks. The elder one read his book during the service and seemed to take no special interest in the fact that his father was up the front talking. And as the months went on Peter had got to know the regular congregations as well as those who came occasionally. He had met regularly with the churchwardens and during the first year had three or four PCC meetings at which he floated ideas about all-age services and maybe starting a children's club. The PCC members made approving noises.

He had established a monthly communion service at The Elms and visited all the PCC members. He had met the chairs of all the parish councils, though he had not yet managed to get to a meeting.

In his second year Peter had begun to take some action about children's work. He had identified one village where there were a number of children who might well come to a service which was geared for children as well as adults, and had met with some of the parents who seemed interested. Then he had hit a problem. The parents were adamant the service needed to be at eleven o'clock. Nine thirty was much too early on a Sunday. But the present service was at nine thirty, and when Peter suggested to the PCC that the time might be changed they were not in support. And when members of the congregation heard that they were not going to have a Holy Communion service on that Sunday but what they called 'a sing-a-long' they were not at all happy. And if he moved the service time to eleven in Barwood then Clound would have to have their service in the evening, and Clound PCC did not like that.

Then Peter had begun to hear of people that he had not visited. They included Mrs Bedridden who had been a regular worshipper at Shalton church until she was taken ill five years ago, and Peter had been here a whole year and had never been to see her once. After all those years that she had come regularly to church as well.

Peter had never heard of Mrs Bedridden. No one had told him she wanted visiting, but when he said this at a PCC meeting umbrage was taken. He should have asked.

He also arranged a wedding at Barwood for the third Sunday in June and wanted the bells rung at two thirty. No one could ring bells at two thirty that day because it was the village fete. Everyone would be at the fete. And the sound of the bells would interfere with the band playing. They always had the Dorminster Town Band to play.

No one had told Peter the village fete was that day. But it was always that day. It always had been.

That was irritating. But when a churchwarden quietly suggested to Peter that some of the congregation had told him they found Peter's children a disturbance during the service it hurt. Were they not meant to be there? Well, people like a quiet atmosphere during the service. And those hassocks which get piled up were sewn by Mrs Wilpott and people don't like seeing them treated like that.

Then the complaints began about what Peter had not done. The two parishioners who had been in Dorminster hospital whom Peter had not visited. No, they did not come to church, but we weren't just concerned about churchgoers, were we? Well, he should have heard that they were in hospital and known that they wanted a visit from the vicar. And the Silver Circle had not seen him for six months. He still had not called on Sir Gerald at Shalton Court, who also never came to church but had been saying just the other day that he had not met the young vicar yet.

Peter was told it was all very well doing school assemblies but what about visiting the Pemble Grove bungalows. The old people matter as well.

And it's all very well changing the services for the young people but they don't stay, do they? It's the old ones that stay. The young ones just move on.

And as for the people who've moved into the new houses at Barwell, they shouldn't expect the villagers to be changing their ways for them. 'They've come into our village. They should join in with our way of doing things before they start asking the church to be changed for them.'

'So,' said the Archdeacon. 'Where does that leave you?'

Peter said, 'Well, I've heard it said that in your first year in a new parish you can't do anything wrong. In the second year you can't do anything right. And in the third year you can't do anything at all. I'm beginning to wonder if it's correct.'

'Ah, but there's another version. In your first year you can't do anything wrong. In your second year you can't do anything right. In your third year you can do what you like!'

'Which one's true?'

'What do you want to do?'

Peter thought for a moment. 'Basically I want the churches to move on. But I don't want to be driving them. I want to move with them.'

'That's hard. If you just want to do your own thing all you need is a thick skin to put up with the criticism.

'If you want a more comfortable life you try and do what's necessary to avoid criticism and maybe try to get a few strokes as well. The church may not go anywhere but at least it'll die happy.

'Or, if you want to try and grow a new church inside the old one you ignore your well-established church members and put up with PCC meetings as an unavoidable pain until you get together enough like-minded people to stage a coup! I don't recommend it, but it's sometimes done.

'But if you want to work with the people who are already members it's harder. We can send you on a course on collaborative work-styles, which would probably help. You'll need to try to understand where they're coming from and you'll need patience. You'll need to talk over how you see things and what you think you can do. And what you can't. The outcome might be good. It might be congregations that build bridges between the different groups within the parishes. Congregations with a wide range of experiences and insights and gifts. It might be churches that are really engaging the gospel with the life of their parishes.

'But, if you want to do that, in the end what happens in the churches depends not only on you but on them as well. Whether they're willing to try to understand you. Whether they're willing to try and work with you. Whether they'll ask themselves what it's realistic to expect from one person. Whether they're willing to think about what the people who don't come to church need as well as themselves. Whether they're willing to leave some of the things that have made them feel safe up till now and take the risk of doing some things differently.

'You can't make all that happen. You can work at it. You can help. But it's also up to them.'

Notes

Chapter 1: **The Country**
1. The Countryside Agency, *The State of the Countryside 2001* (Wetherby, The Countryside Agency, 2001).
2. Howard Newby, *Green and Pleasant Land?* (Harmondsworth, Penguin, 1980), p. 122.
3. Anthony Russell, *The Country Parish* (London, SPCK, 1986), p. 3.
4. Ronald Frankenberg, *Communities in Britain* (Harmondsworth, Penguin, 1966), p. 113.
5. For example, *The State of the Countryside 2001*; Frankenberg, *Communities in Britain*.
6. As in *The State of the Countryside 2001*.
7. ACORA, *Faith in the Countryside* (Worthing, Churchman, 1990), p. 137. For more detail see Anthony Russell, *The Clerical Profession* (London, SPCK, 1980).
8. For example, the report *Mission Shaped Church: church planting and fresh expressions of church in a changing context* (London, Church House Publishing, 2004) was endorsed by the General Synod in February 2004.

Chapter 2: **The Vicar**
1. Anthony Russell, *Groups and Teams in the Countryside* (London, SPCK, 1975); ACORA, *Faith in the Countryside* (Worthing, Churchman, 1990), pp. 165f.
2. *GS Misc 721 Statistics of Licensed Ministers 2002* (London, Church House Publishing, 2003).
3. In Liverpool diocese the clergy have on average a parish population of 6,890 in 1.76 square miles and most have one church. For London the average is 7,190 people, 0.58 square miles and 1 church. In Manchester the average is 7,030 people, 1.54 square miles and 1.3 churches. In the predominantly rural diocese of Carlisle the clergy have on average a parish population of 3,490 spread over 17.95 square miles with 2.5 churches; in Hereford 3,320 people over 17.65 square miles with 4.5 churches; in Lincoln 5,140 people over 14.4 square miles and 3.5 churches; in Exeter 4,210 people over 10.1 square miles and 2.4 churches.

Calculations are from figures in *The Church of England Yearbook 2004* (London, Church House Publishing, 2003).

Chapter 3: Pressures

1. BBC, *A Country Parish* (2003).
2. BBC, *A Seaside Parish* (2004).
3. Douglas Davies *et al.*, *Church and Religion in Rural England* (Edinburgh, T. & T. Clark, 1991), pp. 72f; Neil Burgess, 'The death of the "civilising mission of the churches" – is there a future for ordained pastoral ministry?' in *Modern Believing* (April 2003), 34f (Liverpool, Modern Churchpeople's Union, 2003).
4. Most dioceses have suffragan or area bishops as well as a diocesan. Portsmouth is an exception with one bishop and 102 parish clergy. The ratio of clergy to bishops is not related to whether the diocese is predominantly rural or urban. According to *The Church of England Yearbook 2004* in the largely rural dioceses of Gloucester and Carlisle there are 69 parish clergy per bishop, in Exeter 85 and in Bath and Wells 108. In urban London there are 96, in Liverpool 110 but in Manchester there are 67 (London, Church House Publishing, 2003).
5. Of the 40 diocesan bishops in post when the *Church of England Year Book 2004* went to print 13 had never been a vicar. The others had on average spent 10 years as a vicar (London, Church House Publishing, 2003).
6. Carl Lee and Sarah Horseman, *Affirmation and Accountability: practical suggestions for preventing clergy stress, sickness and ill-health retirement* (Dunsford, The Society of Mary and Martha, 2002).
7. *Affirmation and Accountability*, p. 7.

Chapter 4: The Myth of the Country Parson

1. George Herbert, *A Priest to the Temple or the Country Parson* is available in several editions, for instance in John Tobin (ed.), *George Herbert: the complete English poems* (Harmondsworth, Penguin, 1991).
2. *Country Parson*, ch. 14.
3. *Country Parson* chapter 23
4. From the Prologue to *The Canterbury Tales*.
5. *Country Parson*, ch. 1.
6. *Country Parson*, ch. 23.
7. *Country Parson*, prologue.
8. Anthony Russell, *The Country Parson* (London, SPCK, 1993).
9. George Herbert, *A Priest to the Temple, or, the Country Parson, with selected poems*, Introduction by Ronald Blythe (Norwich, Canterbury Press, 2003).
10. A good source of information on the state of the countryside is The Countryside Agency's annual publication of that name, which is also available on www.countryside.gov.uk.
11. Raymond Williams, *The Country and the City* (Oxford, Oxford University Press, 1975).
12. Rowland Parker, *The Common Stream* (London, Collins, 1975).
13. 'All things bright and beautiful' by Cecil Frances Alexander, verse 3.

Chapter 5: **The Three-dimensional Church**
1. Raymond Fung, *The Isaiah Vision: an ecumenical strategy for congregational evangelism* (Geneva, WCC, 1992).
2. Alpha courses originated at Holy Trinity Church, Brompton, London, SW7 1JA, and are published and promoted by Alpha International at the same address. Emmaus was developed by Stephen Cottrell and others and is published by Church House Publishing, London SW1P 3NZ.
3. John Hencher and Christopher Herbert, *A Place to Dream: a new way of looking at churches and cathedrals* (Leominster, The Orphans Press, 1976; London, Church Information Office, 1976).
4. Kenneth M. Macmorran and Timothy Briden, *A Handbook for Churchwardens and Parochial Church Councillors* (London, Mowbray, 1997), p. 125.

Chapter 6: **Twelve Apostles**
1. There are actually more than a million options. The possible variations in the *Common Worship* Holy Communion Service in Contemporary Language give 13,370 billion possible ways of reading the service, without considering the seasonal variations.

Chapter 7: **The Church and the Vicar**
1. *The Alternative Service Book 1980*, p. 356.
2. Bruce Reed, *The Dynamics of Religion: process and movement in Christian churches* (London, Darton, Longman & Todd, 1978).
3. GS1496 *Formation for Ministry within a Learning Church: the structure and funding of ordination training* (London, Church House Publishing, 2003), known as the Hind Report after the chair of the working party, Bishop John Hind.
4. GS1527 *Review of Clergy Terms of Service: report of the first phase of the work* (London, Ministry Division of the Archbishops' Council, 2004).
5. Advisory Council for the Church's Ministry, *A Strategy for the Church's Ministry* (Westminster, Church Information Office, 1983), known as the Tiller Report.
6. John Tiller, *Tiller Ten Years on: changing prospects for the church's ministry* (Bramcote, Grove Books, 1993).

Chapter 8: **Working It Out Together**
1. Bruce Reed, *The Dynamics of Religion: process and movement in Christian churches* ((London, Darton, Longman & Todd, 1978), pp. 79ff.
2. Canon E1 of *The Canons of the Church of England* (London, Church House Publishing, 2000) refers to the office and work of churchwardens but it is very general. There is more guidance available for churchwardens in handbooks such as James Behrens, *Practical Parish Management: a guide for every parish* (Leominster, Gracewing, 1998) and Martin Dudley and Virginia Rounding, *Churchwarden – A Survival Guide: the office and role of the churchwarden in the twenty first century* (London, SPCK, 2003).
3. Canon C24.

4. See, for example, George Lovell and Catherine Widdicombe, *Churches and Communities: an approach to development in the local church* (London, Search Press, 1978); Loughlan Sofield ST and Carroll Juliano SHCJ, *Collaborative Ministry: skills and guidelines* (Notre Dame Ind., Ave Maria Press, 1987); T. R. and M. Batten, *The Non-Directive Approach* (London, Avec, 1988).

Chapter 9: Bigger Circles

1. *Mind the Gap: integrated continuing ministerial education for the Church's ministers* (London, Church House Publishing, 2003).
2. Leslie Paul, *The Deployment and Payment of the Clergy* (London, Church Information Office, 1964), known as the Paul Report.
3. Advisory Council for the Church's Ministry, *A Strategy for the Church's Ministry* (Westminster, Church Information Office, 1983), known as the Tiller Report.
4. Rural Theology Association, The Vicarage, Rudston, Driffield, East Yorkshire, YO25 4XA.
5. The Arthur Rank Centre, National Agricultural Centre, Stoneleigh Park, Warwickshire, CV8 2LZ.
6. Gerd Theissen, *The First Followers of Jesus: a sociological analysis of the earliest Christianity* (London, SCM Press, 1978).

Chapter 10: Life and God

1. Douglas Davies *et al.*, *Church and Religion in Rural England* (Edinburgh, T. & T. Clark, 1991), pp. 72ff.
2. Anthony Russell, *The Country Parson* (London, SPCK, 1993).
3. Avery Dulles SJ, *Models of the Church: a critical assessment of the church in all its aspects* (Dublin, Gill & Macmillan, 1976).
4. Quoted by John Carden, *Morning, Noon and Night: prayers and meditations from the Third World* (London, CMS, 1976). I have made every effort to trace the copyright holder but so far without success. I apologise for this and would welcome an opportunity to communicate with the Companions of Brother Lawrence.
5. The phrase originates with D. W. Winnicott whose work underpins Bruce Reed's theory of the dynamics of religion. John McLeod, *An Introduction to Counselling* (Buckingham, Open University Press, 1993).
6. Jennifer Thomson, as quoted by her daughter Elizabeth. Jennifer also said she applied the same principle to gardening.

Chapter 11: Work, Vocation and Justice

1. *The Way Ahead: Church of England schools in the new millennium* (London, Church House Publishing, 2003), known as the Dearing Report after its chair, Lord Dearing.
2. For a development of the implications of this for the way the Church of England operates see Neil Burgess, 'Podium: pastoral care and the church' in *Modern Believing* (July 2002), 43f (London, Modern Churchpeople's Union, 2002).

Bibliography

Bible references
Unless specified otherwise all scripture quotations are from the New
Revised Standard Version Bible © 1989 by the Division of Christian
Education of the National Council of the Churches of Christ in the USA and
are used by permission. All rights reserved.

Studies and background documents
Advisory Council for the Church's Ministry, The, *A Strategy for the Church's
Ministry* (the Tiller Report), Westminster, Church Information Office, 1983.
Alternative Service Book 1980, The, London, Central Board of Finance of the
Church of England, 1980.
Archbishops' Commission on Rural Areas, The, *Faith in the Countryside*,
Worthing, Churchman, 1990.
Archbishops' Council, The, *The Canons of the Church of England*, London,
Church House Publishing, 2000.
— *Church Representation Rules*, London, Church House Publishing, 2001.
— *Church of England Year Book 2003*, London, Church House Publishing, 2003.
— *GS1496 Formation for Ministry within a Learning Church: the structure and
funding of ordination training* (the Hind Report), London, Church House
Publishing, 2003.
— *GS Misc 721 Statistics of Licensed Ministers 2002*, London, Church House
Publishing, 2003.
— *Mind the Gap: integrated continuing ministerial education for the church's
ministers*, London, Church House Publishing, 2003.
— *The Way Ahead: Church of England schools in the new millennium* (the
Dearing Report), London, Church House Publishing, 2003.
— *GS1527 Review of Clergy Terms of Service: report of the first phase of the work*,
London, Ministry Division of the Archbishops' Council, 2004.
— *Mission-Shaped Church: church planting and fresh expressions of church in a
changing context* (the Cray Report), London, Church House Publishing,
2004.
ARCIC II, *Salvation and the Church: an agreed statement by the Anglican–Roman
Catholic International Commission*, London, Church House Publishing, 1987.

Bibliography

Assagioli, Roberto, *Psychosynthesis: a manual of principles and techniques*, London, Harper Collins, 1993.

Batten, T. R. and M., *The Non-Directive Approach*, London, Avec, 1988.

Blythe, Ronald, Introduction, in George Herbert, *A Priest to the Temple, or, the Country Parson, with selected poems*, Norwich, Canterbury Press, 2003.

Book of Common Prayer, The.

Bowden, Andrew, *Ministry in the Countryside:* a *model for the future*, 2nd edition, London, Continuum, 2003.

Bradley, Ian, *Colonies of Heaven: Celtic models for today's church*, London, Darton, Longman & Todd, 2000.

Briggs, Asa, *A Social History of England*, London, Weidenfeld & Nicolson, 1983.

Burgess, Neil, 'Podium: pastoral care and the church' in *Modern Believing* (July 2002), London, Modern Churchpeople's Union, 2002.

— 'The death of the "civilising mission of the churches" – is there a future for ordained pastoral ministry?' in *Modern Believing* (April 2003), Liverpool, Modern Churchpeople's Union, 2003.

Chadwick, Owen, *The Reformation*, Harmondsworth, Penguin, 1964.

— *The Victorian Church*, 2 vols., London, A. & C. Black, 1970.

Chaucer, Geoffrey, *The Canterbury Tales*, The World's Classics edition, London, Oxford University Press, 1906.

Coate, Mary Anne, *Clergy Stress: the hidden conflicts in ministry*, London, SPCK, 1989.

Common Worship, London, Church House Publishing, 2000.

Countryside Agency, The, *The State of the Countryside 2001*, Wetherby, The Countryside Agency, 2001.

Cragg, G. R., *The Church and the Age of Reason 1648–1789*, Harmondsworth, Penguin, 1960.

Crawford, Peter, *The Living Isle: a natural history of Britain and Ireland*, London, BBC, 1985.

Davie, Grace, *Religion in Britain since 1945: believing without belonging*, Oxford, Blackwell, 1994.

— *Religion in Modern Europe: a memory mutates*, Oxford, Oxford University Press, 2000.

Davies, Douglas *et al.*, *Church and Religion in Rural England*, Edinburgh, T. & T. Clark, 1991.

Department of the Environment, Transport and the Regions, *Our Countryside, the Future: a fair deal for rural England*, London, HMSO, 2000.

Dewar, Francis, *Called or Collared? an alternative approach to vocation*, London, SPCK, 1991.

Dulles SJ, Avery, *Models of the Church: a critical assessment of the church in all its aspects*, Dublin, Gill & Macmillan, 1976.

Finney, John, *Understanding Leadership*, London, Darton, Longman & Todd, 1989.

Francis, Leslie J., *Rural Anglicanism: a future for young Christians?*, London, Collins, 1985.

— *Partnership in Rural Education: Church schools and teacher attitudes*, London, Collins, 1986.

— *The Country Parson*, Leominster, Fowler Wright, 1989.

Francis, Leslie *et al.*, *Making Contact: Christian nurture, family worship and church growth*, London, Collins, 1986.

Frankenberg, Ronald, *Communities in Britain*, Harmondsworth, Penguin, 1966.

Fung, Raymond, *The Isaiah Vision: an ecumenical strategy for congregational evangelism*, Geneva, WCC, 1992.

Gill, Robin, *The Myth of the Empty Church*, London, SPCK, 1993.

Gilley, Sheridan and Sheils, W. J. (eds.), *A History of Religion in Britain*, Oxford, Blackwell, 1994.

Green, Robin, *Only Connect: worship and liturgy from the perspective of pastoral care*, London, Darton, Longman & Todd, 1987.

Greenwood, Robin, 'Mission, community and the local church' in *Crucible* (July 2001), London, Board of Social Responsibility, 2001.

— *Transforming Church: liberating structures for ministry*, London, SPCK, 2003.

Groome, Thomas H., *Christian Religious Education: sharing our story and vision*, San Francisco, Harper & Row, 1980.

Herbert, George, *A Priest to the Temple or the Country Parson* in Tobin, John (ed.), *George Herbert: the complete English poems*, Harmondsworth, Penguin, 1991.

Hoskins, W. G., *The Making of the English Landscape*, Harmondsworth, Penguin, 1970.

Inter-Anglican Theological and Doctrinal Commission, *For the Sake of the Kingdom: God's Church and the new creation*, London, Church House Publishing, 1986.

Jinkins, Michael, *Transformational Ministry: church leadership and the way of the cross*, Edinburgh, St Andrew Press, 2002.

Küng, Hans, *The Church*, London, Search Press, 1968.

Lawson, John and Silver, Harold, *A Social History of Education in Britain*, London, Methuen, 1973.

Leadbetter, Shannon, 'Vocation and our understanding of God' in *Modern Believing* (October 2001), London, Modern Churchpeople's Union, 2001.

Lewis, Richard and Talbot-Ponsonby, Andrew (eds.), *The People, the Land and the Church*, Hereford, Hereford Diocesan Board of Finance, 1987.

Lindberg, Carter, *The European Reformations*, Oxford, Blackwell, 1996.

Lovell, George, *Consultancy, Ministry and Mission: a handbook for practitioners and work consultants in Christian organisations*, London, Burns & Oates, 2000.

Lovell, George and Widdicombe, Catherine, *Churches and Communities: an approach to development in the local church*, London, Search Press, 1978.

McLeod, John, *An Introduction to Counselling*, Buckingham, Open University Press, 1993.

McLeod, Hugh, *Religion and the People of Western Europe*, Oxford, Oxford University Press, 1997.

Moltmann, Jürgen, *The Church in the Power of the Spirit*, London, SCM Press, 1977.

— *The Open Church: invitation to a messianic lifestyle*, London, SCM Press, 1978.

Moody, Christopher, *Eccentric Ministry: pastoral care and leadership in the parish*, London, Darton, Longman & Todd, 1992.

Moran, Gabriel, *Education toward Adulthood: religion and lifelong learning*, Dublin, Gill & Macmillan, 1980.

— *Religious Education Development: images for the future*, Minneapolis, Winston Press, 1983.

Nelson, John (ed.), *Management and Ministry – appreciating contemporary issues*, Norwich, Canterbury Press, 1996.

Newby, Howard, *Green and Pleasant Land?*, Harmondsworth, Penguin, 1980.

Parker, Rowland, *The Common Stream*, London, Collins, 1975.

Paul, Leslie, *The Deployment and Payment of the Clergy* (the Paul Report), London, Church Information Office, 1964.

— *A Church by Daylight: a reappraisement of the Church of England and its future*, London, Geoffrey Chapman, 1973.

Peterson, Eugene H., *The Gift: reflections on Christian ministry*, London, Collins, 1995.

Poulton, John, *Fresh Air: a vision for the future of the rural church*, Basingstoke, Marshall Pickering, 1985.

Rackham, Oliver, *The History of the Countryside*, London, Weidenfeld & Nicolson, 1995.

Ramsey, Michael, *The Christian Priest Today*, revised edition, London, SPCK, 1985.

Reed, Bruce, *The Dynamics of Religion: process and movement in Christian churches*, London, Darton, Longman & Todd, 1978.

Reed, Esther D., 'Labour law and the employment status of the clergy', *Crucible* (July 2003), London, SCM Press, 2003.

Roose-Evans, James, *Passages of the Soul: rediscovering the importance of rituals in everyday life*, Shaftesbury, Element, 1994.

Russell, Anthony, *The Village in Myth and Reality*, London, Chester House, 1975.

— *Groups and Teams in the Countryside*, London, SPCK, 1975.

— *The Clerical Profession*, London, SPCK, 1980.

— *The Country Parish*, London, SPCK, 1986.

— *The Country Parson*, London, SPCK, 1993.

Shoard, Marian, *The Theft of the Countryside*, London, Temple Smith, 1980.

— *This Land Is Our Land*, London, Harper Collins, 1987.

Southern, R. W., *Western Society and the Church in the Middle Ages*, Harmondsworth, Penguin, 1970.

Theissen, Gerd, *The First Followers of Jesus: a sociological analysis of the earliest Christianity*, London, SCM Press, 1978.

Thomas, Richard, *Counting People In: changing the way we think about membership and the church*, London, SPCK, 2003.

Tiller, John, *Tiller Ten Years On: changing prospects for the church's ministry*, Bramcote, Grove Books, 1993.

Tiller, John, with Birchall, Mark, *The Gospel Community and its Leadership*, Basingstoke, Marshall Pickering, 1987.

Tobin, John (ed.), *George Herbert: the complete English poems*, Harmondsworth, Penguin, 1991.

van de Weyer, Robert, *Island Vision: prophets, pastors and pilgrims of the English Church*, Basingstoke, Marshall Pickering, 1988.

— *The Country Church*, London, Darton, Longman & Todd, 1991.

Vidler, Alec R., *The Church in an Age of Revolution*, Harmondsworth, Penguin, 1961.

Walrond-Skinner, Sue, 'Pastoral care – the Church's essential task' in *Modern Believing* (January 2002), London, Modern Churchpeople's Union, 2002.

Warren, Yvonne, *The Cracked Pot: the state of today's Anglican parish clergy*, Stowmarket, Kevin Mayhew, 2002.

West, Frank, *The Country Parish Today and Tomorrow*, 2nd edition, London, SPCK, 1964.

Whitlock, Ralph, *A Short History of Farming in Britain*, Wakefield, EP Publishing, 1977.

Williams, Raymond, *The Country and the City*, Oxford, Oxford University Press, 1975.

Workbooks

Alexander, Mike and Martineau, Jeremy, *So the Vicar's Leaving: making the most of an interregnum*, revised edition, Norwich, Canterbury Press, 2002.

Ammerman, Nancy T. *et al.* (eds.), *Studying Congregations: a new handbook*, Nashville, Abingdon Press, 1998.

Baumohl, Anton, *Making Adult Disciples: learning and teaching in the local church*, London, Scripture Union, 1984.

Behrens, James, *Practical Parish Management: a guide for every parish*, Leominster, Gracewing, 1998.

Bergin, Eilis and Fitzgerald, Eddie, *An Enneagram Guide: a spirituality of love in brokenness*, Dublin, SDB Media, 1993.

Burgess, Ruth, *A Book of Blessings and How to Write Your Own*, Glasgow, Wild Goose Publications, 2001.

— *Friends and Enemies: a book of short prayers and some ways to write your own*, Glasgow, Wild Goose Publications, 2003.

Carden, John, *Morning, Noon and Night: prayers and meditations from the Third World*, London, CMS, 1976.

Dudley, Martin and Rounding, Virginia, *Churchwarden – A Survival Guide: the office and role of the churchwarden in the twenty first century*, London, SPCK, 2003.

Francis, Leslie J. and Martineau, Jeremy, *Rural Praise: a parish workbook for worship in the country church*, Leominister, Fowler Wright, 1996.

— *A Parish Workbook for Welcoming Visitors to the Country Church*, Stoneleigh Park, ACORA Publishing, 2001.

— *Rural Mission: a parish workbook for developing the mission of the local church*, Stoneleigh Park, ACORA Publishing, 2002.

Francis, L. J., Littler, K. and Martineau, J., *Rural Ministry: a parish workbook for lay ministry in the local church*, Stoneleigh Park, ACORA, 2000.

Goldsmith, Malcolm and Wharton, Martin, *Knowing Me, Knowing You: exploring personality type and temperament*, London, SPCK, 1993.

Green, Laurie, *Let's Do Theology: a pastoral cycle resource book* London, Mowbray, 1990.

Greenwood, Robin, *The Ministry Team Handbook: local church as partnership*, London, SPCK, 2000.

Grundy, Malcolm, *What They Don't Teach You at Theological College: a practical guide to life in the ministry*, Norwich, Canterbury Press, 2003.

Hencher, John and Herbert, Christopher, *A Place to Dream: a new way of looking at churches and cathedrals*, Leominster, The Orphans Press, 1976; London, Church Information Office, 1976.

Hinton, Jeanne and Price, Peter B., *Changing Communities: church from the grassroots*, London, CTBI, 2003.

Lee, Carl and Horseman, Sarah, *Affirmation and Accountability: practical suggestions for preventing clergy stress, sickness and ill-health retirement*, Dunsford, The Society of Mary and Martha, 2002.

Macmorran, Kenneth M. and Briden, Timothy, *A Handbook for Churchwardens and Parochial Church Councillors*, London, Continuum, 2001.

Martineau, Jeremy, *Turning the Sod: a workbook on the multi-parish benefice*, Stoneleigh Park, ACORA Publishing, 1995.

Methodist Church, The, *Presence: a workbook to help promote and sustain an effective Christian presence in villages*, London, Methodist Church Publishing, 2004.

Napier, Charles and Hamilton-Brown, J., *A New Workbook on Rural Evangelism*, Blandford Forum, Parish & People, 1994.

Perry, David W. (ed.), *Homegrown Christian Education: planning and programming for Christian education in the local congregation*, New York, Seabury Press, 1979.

Pitchford, John, *An ABC for the PCC: a handbook for church council members*, London, Continuum, 2003.

Richter, Philip, *God's Here and Now: contexts of the ministry of the people of God*, London, Darton, Longman & Todd, 1999.

Riso, Don Richard, *The Enneagram: discovering your personality type*, London, Harper Collins, 1995.

Savigear, Elfrida, *The Servant Church: organising rural social care*, Stoneleigh Park, ACORA Publishing, 1996).

Sofield, Loughlan and Juliano, Carroll, *Collaborative Ministry: skills and guidelines*, Notre Dame Ind., Ave Maria Press, 1987.

Westerhoff, John H. and Willimon, William H., *Liturgy and Learning through the Life Cycle*, New York, Seabury, 1980.

Wild Goose Resource Group, *A Wee Worship Book, 4th Incarnation*, Glasgow, Wild Goose Publications, 1999.

Television
BBC, *A Country Parish*, 2003.
BBC, *A Seaside Parish*, 2004.

Index